21st Century Relationship Guide

Communicate Your Way to True Intimacy

21st Century Relationship Guide

Communicate Your Way to True Intimacy

By Des Coroy

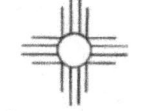

The Zia Press

The Zia Press
www.theziapress.com

Copyright © Des Coroy, 2014

All rights reserved. No part of this publication, either in part or in whole, may be reproduced, transmitted or utilized in any form, by any means, electronic, photographic, or mechanical, including photocopying, recording or by any information storage system, without permission in writing from the author, except for brief quotations embodied in literary articles and reviews.

This book is dedicated to:

My mother, **Eloise**,
who first taught me
about love & how to
live life to the fullest.

You, my fellow traveler in time.
May the ideas enclosed within
serve you as your guiding star
in your journeys through the seas
of **Love.**

Table of Contents

Preface 8
Introduction-How To Use This Book 13

PART I - Practical Communication Techniques 23
Chapter 1 - Raise the Level of Your Expectations 25
Chapter 2 - Communicate or Disintegrate 34
Chapter 3 - The Gift of Listening 44
Chapter 4 - The Talking Stick 51
Chapter 5 - Truth, the Lifeblood of Love 61
Chapter 6 - Entering the War Zone 69
Chapter 7 - Withholds 81

PART II - Supportive Relationship Concepts 87
Chapter 8 - Emotional Time Bombs 89
Chapter 9 - My Partner, My Mirror 107
Chapter 10 - Forgiving the Past 128
Chapter 11 - No-No Land Attractions & Affairs, the Ultimate Taboo 141
Chapter 12 - Women and Men - Two Peas in a Human Pod 161
Chapter 13 - Outside Interference 184
Chapter 14 - Romance and Recreation 206
Chapter 15 - Closing Ceremonies 213
Chapter 16 - Serial Soulmates 245

Chapter 17 – Attracting a Life Partner 251
Chapter 18 – New Vision 259
Appendix 1 – Children and the Talking Stick 263
Appendix 2 – The Talking Stick Method 2 266
Acknowledgments 268

Preface

In addition to breakthrough innovations in scientific knowledge and technology, the 20th century will also be remembered for producing a generation of souls who radically changed the form and substance of intimate relationships.

Along with many individuals from my generation, when it comes to intimate relationships I've had a considerable amount of personal experience. I grew up in the "flower-child generation" of the late '60s and early '70s of the last century. We were the baby boomer generation who broke the molds of conventional relationships by choosing to experiment with "free love".

We were truly the relationship revolutionaries of our era. We rebelled against traditional society's strict adherence to marriage as the only suitable form for an intimate relationship and we initiated the concept of cohabitation without seeking religious or government sanctioning. Today, two unmarried individuals living together as a couple are fully accepted as an appropriate form of relationship but at the time it was a revolutionary idea.

Because we were collectively pioneering the cutting edge of love, many of our experiments in relationships failed. We were a courageous bunch of souls. As soon as we were knocked down in love, we would get back on the merry-go-round and keep trying again and again to get it right. In the process of trying to find the right formula for a new and more fulfilling type of relationship, our quest for free love actually was not free and cost us regular payments of emotional pain. Perhaps the "baby boomers" should more properly be called the "divorce boomers."

However, we were determined not to make the same mistakes as many of our parents who remained in lifeless, unfulfilling unions for the sake of the societal ideal. Hence, many of us spent a lot of years continuing to search for a better way.

As a young man, I signed up as an eager explorer on the path of relationships. Over the years I have been privileged to share a deep love with six extraordinary women in various forms of intimate relationships, ranging from traditional marriage to cohabitation. I have been blessed with three magnificent daughters — Kelly, Crystall and Vanessa —from two marriages......

Perhaps you prefer learning about relationship skills from someone who has been in one love relationship in his or her life. However, I ask you these questions. If you needed the services of a brain surgeon, would you search for a young surgeon just out of med school who is eagerly awaiting his very first cut? Or, if you were going to fly on a jet from Los Angeles to Sydney, would you want to have an experienced pilot who has logged lots of hours flying in a variety of different aircraft? If experience counts in relationships, then I can assure you that I am a competent 'pilot'.

I may not be able to tell you exactly what path of relationship to travel on. However I certainly can point out to you what paths not to go on!

Some of the experiences of my education were joyful beyond measure while many other experiences presented me with hard and painful lessons to work out. The primary reason I continued to have to learn such difficult lessons in my life was a lack of awareness of my inner nature and a total lack of communication skills within those relationships.

When I was a youth, I never attended any "Everything you've always wanted to learn about relationships but were afraid to ask" class on how to have a successful partnership. Like most of us, I learned my lessons about love through on-the-job training. The old tried and true method of education about love called trial and error was my favored approach with a heavy emphasis on error. Of course, it was not my error because blame was the name of the game I played.

I wasn't aware of how important it was to tell the truth to my partner or how to fight fairly. Listening was not a word I heard, nor did I possess an ability to communicate effectively in my relationships. The mutual lack of relationship skills led to inevitable problems, which eventually wrecked the partnership.

After a while, I wondered why I repeatedly found myself stranded on the reefs of relationships. Over time I started to question my contribution to the challenging relationship realities confronting me again and again. I finally realized that the reason I was experiencing trouble in my relationships was because of the choices I was making, both conscious and unconscious. When I truly understood that my inner thoughts, beliefs and feelings about relationships created the actual experiences in my life, I discovered a map which could guide me away from those reefs of pain and toward the shores of joy.

As I learned to accept personal responsibility for my relationship experiences by making positive choices, the pattern of difficulties started to change and I began to enjoy more and more harmony in my associations with others.

I began to utilize the power of truth more in my life along with developing more effective communication skills. I started practicing these new listening skills with the people in my life and I noticed an immediate improvement in the quality of those relationships.

Encouraged by the positive results in my life, I became an avid student of relationships. Through my studies I discovered that it's impossible to have a healthy relationship with another individual if you don't have a healthy relationship with your own self. It was a time in my life when I discovered my basic emotional needs and desires and learned how to provide for those needs without depending on another person to do it for me. Even though I spent considerable time without a relationship, for the first time in my life I truly enjoyed my own company because I was learning self acceptance.

Over the years, I continued my relationship studies by attending numerous seminars and reading a great number of books on the subject. Eventually my intense interest in the inner workings of relationships motivated me to serve others by developing my gift of intuition to a point where I was able to counsel others in a professional capacity. I wanted to share what I learned with others because I knew that if I could learn to improve my previously nonexistent relationship skills, then, with the will and desire to do so, anyone would be able to.

In my time serving as a Relationship Explorer & Guide, I have counseled thousands of couples over the years and, without a doubt, in most relationships the number one problem between partners is a lack of effective communication skills. Poor communication between a couple increases stress in their relationship because of their inability to talk about the day-to-day problems of life. Eventually, the quality of the relationship begins to disintegrate.

The ideas in this book are presented to you as a distillation of my personal relationship explorations, the wisdom of my teachers, and the knowledge gained from the relationship experiences of many individuals I have previously counseled.

Every book is written from the point of view of its author. The concepts in this book about relationships are written from my personal point of view. Because of your own individual view, you may agree with some of the ideas presented on these pages and disagree with others. My request to you is to test out the validity of these concepts in your own personal relationship.

With pleasure, I offer you these insights as a possible map which you can use to bypass the hidden reefs of relationships and consequently avoid many obstacles along your path.

Bon voyage my friend,
Des

Introduction—How To Use This Book

The Quest for Fulfillment

Love alone can unite living beings so as to complete and fulfill them...for it alone joins them by what is deepest in themselves.
  Pierre Teilhard De Chardin (1881-1955),
  French Christian mystic, author.

Most people want more passion, joy, communication, fun and, ultimately, fulfillment in their relationship. The question is: Are you willing to put time and effort into achieving those goals? Are you committed to the process of personal growth in your own life?

Everything in this material universe requires regular maintenance or it begins to disintegrate. Relationships are no exception. Most people put a lot of hours and effort into their careers, constantly trying to improve performance levels. When it comes to their relationship, I think it's safe to say that the average person puts very little constructive time into improving the levels of communication, intimacy, and romance within their partnership. How many hours of effort a week do you put into improving the quality of your relationship?

Fulfillment, like most things of value, will not be handed to you on a silver platter. It's a quality worth striving for every day of your life. Fulfillment in your relationship is like the sweet fruit at the end of the branch. You have to crawl out there on the limb to get it. It takes skill, balance and a desire to taste its nectar. Unfortunately, many people settle for the tasteless fruit of mediocrity in their relationships because they are unwilling to take a risk and climb out on that emotional limb.

Love brings you together. It doesn't provide you with the communication skills that will assist you in making it grow.

No one taught you how to effectively communicate within your relationships. You probably were not taught how to argue fairly with others, listen more effectively to them or to speak your truth no matter what the consequences. When you left your family home, you weren't given a how-to manual on relationships. In fact, your parents probably didn't tell you very much at all about how to live in harmony with another human being because they probably didn't know themselves.

Some people change their ways when they see the light, others when they feel the heat.
Caroline Schoeder.

Initially we learn about relationships through our role models — our parents. Sometimes they got it right but more than likely they were struggling with the same issues as everyone else. So where did you learn your interpersonal skills? Unfortunately, most of your lessons about relationships are acquired in the arena of your own personal experience. Learning through trial and error is certainly one way of acquiring knowledge but it's often a painful process.

This book has specific practical knowledge which will assist you in avoiding many of the difficult trial and error experiences that may arise in your own intimate relationship.

There are two major reasons why many intimate relationships don't work — incompatibility and poor communication skills, and oftentimes both.

Your positive application of the tools described can make a huge difference in the quality of communications between you and your partner. In addition, by improving communication overall compatibility often improves in your relationship.

The beginning of this book gets right into practicalities by giving you tools that you can use straight away. It has been written with the Talking Stick as its core. Based on an ancient Native American tradition, it's a powerful communication instrument that will assist you in implementing the processes explained later.

There are two clear intentions embedded on these pages:
1. The primary intention is to provide you and your partner with clear insights and practical techniques for creating dynamic communication breakthroughs in your relationship. These breakthroughs can lead to a depth of intimacy and fulfillment that few attain.
2. The secondary reason is to provide you with tools to assist you in gaining clarity on whether it is in your best interest as a couple to continue your relationship in its present form. In addition, if you discover that it is time to let it go, this book assists in you saying your goodbyes with as much grace as possible.

I realize that the second intention just mentioned above will go against some individuals' personal belief that all relationships, and especially marriages, should survive until "death do us part." And even though those individuals have the intention to live together for a lifetime, unfortunately they may be faced with the reality of separating, letting go and moving on. Then the chapter called Closing Ceremonies may be of assistance in teaching them how to let go of their relationship with dignity and grace.

Unlike most relationship books, this one is not designed to assist you in super-gluing your relationship together at all costs. My reasons will be explained in later pages.

This book is about you taking personal responsibility for the choices you make in your relationship. It is not for everyone. The ideas espoused will precipitate division as much as union in relationships. Many individuals are not ready or willing to consciously participate in the process of improving the quality of their relationship. If you are not prepared to accept personal responsibility for your contribution to any issues present in your relationship and you are stuck with blaming your partner for all the problems, then you're probably not at a point where this book can assist you.

On the other hand, if you were attracted to these pages, and you realize that it takes two to tango, then there is a strong probability that you're ready to move to a new level of personal fulfilment in your relationship. If you truly desire to gain greater understanding and resolution of the day-to-day issues confronting you in your relationship, then perhaps this book will bring you the clarity that you need. It will expose you to concepts that may forever alter your view on relationships and serve as a catalyst for positive change within your union.

90-day invitation for you to create dynamic breakthroughs in your relationship

Social scientists tell us that it takes approximately 90 days of focused effort to change personal habits. I assure you that if you and your partner fully participate in practicing the concepts within this book for 90 days, you will see a dramatic improvement in the quality and clarity of your communications within your relationship. I am extending an invitation to you to value your relationship enough to put a 90-day effort into creating dynamic breakthroughs on every level of your relationship.

If you are not completely happy with the way you and your partner are interacting and you feel there is room for improvement, then investing three months of your life toward regenerating your relationship is well worth the effort. It takes very little time to use these concepts and we always have time for the things that we value.

You may discover that you and your partner have been withholding emotions from each other within your relationship, and you can expect a little friction as those feelings are expressed. The techniques within this book are designed to assist you in moving through any friction with the minimum amount of generated "heat."

As you and your partner move through these chapters, you'll experience varying levels of agreement and disagreement about issues that will surface in your relationship. Don't be concerned if you feel frustration occasionally, because the book was written with the intention of stimulating constructive change in your relationship. Feeling a little anger from time to time can positively assist you in shifting rigid emotional patterns which have kept your relationship stagnant. When you notice that one of you gets stuck on a chapter, closes the book and emotionally withdraws from the process, it's usually a sign that the issues being discussed in that particular chapter are the very ones that need to be addressed.

When you look deeper, you'll most likely discover fears about the subject being discussed which are sabotaging your progress. It's very important when reaching this crisis point to persevere in your efforts by pushing through your fear. Being vulnerable enough to share your fears with each other will assist you in releasing them and carrying on with the book.

> A nail is driven out by another nail.
> Habit is overcome by habit.
> Desiderius Erasmus (c.1466-1536),
> Dutch humanist.

When you hang in there for 90 days, the investment of your time and effort will reward both of you with greater communication skills, increased clarity about each other's needs and a much greater chance of regenerating the passion in your relationship. However, it will only work if you both are fully committed to being absolutely fair with each other in the communication process. It will not work if one of you wants to maintain dominance and control in your communications with the other. How could it? And yet if you are both committed to learning new ways of hearing and being heard, then you both can experience a totally new way of safely communicating your deepest truth to each other and achieve a deep understanding of the other's point of view.

You may find that your partner is not interested in participating in improving the communication level of your relationship. If so, then please do not attempt to force him or her to do so because the commitment needed for growth just isn't present. The very fact that your partner chooses not to participate usually indicates that at this particular point you each want different things out of your relationship.

By all means if you want to continue reading without your partner's involvement, please do so because the ideas within will give you greater understanding about the difficulties in your relationship. Quite often, one partner choosing to improve their communication skills will serve as a catalyst for the non-participating partner to eventually get on board.

Read Part 1 within two weeks

I suggest that you and your partner set a timeline of reading Part 1 of this book within a two-week period either by sharing one book or by each having your own copy to read. When you have completed Part 1, then you both can begin your suggested 90-day exploration into improving communication by using the communication techniques which will be fully explained in the subsequent chapters. After the initial reading of Part 1, I suggest that each partner complete the book by reading Part 2, which contains concepts that will support the processes of communication initiated between you and your partner.

As you progress through this book, you will come across three written agreements which you will be requested to sign. It's important that you and your partner physically sign the agreements, showing your commitment to the process of learning new communication techniques.

Basic premise:
You're here to learn the lesson of love

You can search throughout the entire universe for someone who is more deserving of your love and affection than you are yourself, and that person is not to be found anywhere. You, yourself, as much as anybody in the entire universe, deserve your love and affection.

Gautama Buddha

On this planet, the most advanced school where you acquire this lesson about love is your relationships. As we live in possibly the most materialistic age ever on Earth, we lose sight of this primary truth. The basis of this book, the cornerstone of truth which prompted me to write it, is that we are all spiritual beings living here for a short while as human beings. I believe that before we were born on this planet, our essence, soul, spirit, the "I Am" of us, existed somewhere in a different form than your present body.

I trust that the reason our spirits envelop ourselves in the density of a human body is to experience growth, knowledge and, most importantly, to learn the lessons of opening our hearts to the free expression and receiving of love. How many more years do you think you have left to live? Ten years? Twenty years? Forty years? Even if you answered seventy years, it is still a blink of the eye compared to a 6 million-year-old piece of rock.

You are a spiritual being in a costume called the human body. Enjoy the party!

The spirituality of which I am writing is that every moment of your existence you are a walking, talking, and divine manifestation of pure life force while here on Earth. The very fiber of your being is woven together with the strands of love. There is no area of your life that is not spiritual. All life is your spiritual playground.

It often doesn't feel like it, does it? That's because we forget who we are the moment we are born on this materially dense little planet. Because of our collective amnesia, we get our priorities confused and create a world whose first priority is spending, buying, and obsessing about money and material possessions. If you doubt this statement, just ask yourself how many times a day you think about money, either getting it, losing it, or not having it. Then ask yourself how many times a day you think about love, how you can give and receive more of it today. No comparison between the two, as money wins hands down.

Somehow I know that at the moment when we leave this life, the day of our transition when we move onto the next great adventure, the last thought that we will experience will not be what money we are leaving behind, or what we may or may not have accomplished. The only thing we will be thinking about at that moment is how much love we shared, received, and experienced during our short stay on Earth.

Intimate relationships are the superhighway of spiritual growth

So what does all of this have to do with relationships, you may ask? Relationships of all kinds, and most importantly intimate relationships, are where we grind out our rough corners and absorb lessons about love. Many of these lessons are deeply painful and many are joyful beyond measure.

The pain descends from our fear, our unawareness, and the lack of skills in communicating our hopes, fears, dreams and needs to each other. The joy arises from our moments of true communion and contact with the souls of others when we open our hearts to the vivifying power of pure love.

Of all the spiritual or personal growth paths, the path of intimate relationships is potentially the fastest one of all when two conscious beings mutually commit to the process of their individual and mutual growth. The dynamics of two human beings in day-to-day intimacy with each other brings to light the most noble aspects and qualities of their inner selves and it also exposes the darkest, most destructive traits as well.

It's a fast path and it can also be a very difficult one.

Why do you think that most great spiritual leaders were single? Probably because it's a whole lot easier sitting on a mountaintop by yourself contemplating the mysteries of the universe than to deal with the reality of another human being. I wonder how they would have fared if they had entered into a real human partnership and tested out those lofty spiritual concepts in the down-to-earth coliseum of life called intimate relationships.

Relationships are the swiftest and can be the most challenging spiritual path of all. When it's working and all things are flowing, it's pure bliss. When it's not happening according to plan, your relationship can become the repository of pure pain.

The oyster needs the speck of sand to irritate it just enough to produce the beauty and wonder of a pearl. Likewise, in your intimate relationships, the inevitable feelings of disharmony which arise act as the emotional "sand" required for change. In the sacred vessel of your relationship this disharmony serves as the friction required to transform your darker feelings of anger and fear into "pearls" of love, compassion and ecstasy.

Go easy on yourself

The ideas here are targets to aim for and ideals to aspire toward. As you progress through this book, you may discover aspects of yourself that you recognize. You may become aware of personal behaviors that are causing problems for you in your relationship.

Whenever you discover behaviors that you would like to change, then do so gently and patiently. Please avoid allowing your inner critic to beat you up about any perceived lack of relationships skills. Don't judge yourself for not knowing something you were never taught. Accept that you just didn't know a different way until now.

This is a time on Earth when we are all learning these lessons together. We all trip up from time to time, so please approach the coming changes with patience, acceptance and love. You will learn your lessons of love through pain or through joy. What is your choice?

Many couples are learning their relationship lessons by traveling on the difficult path of unconsciousness. They're still growing in their ability to give and receive love. It's just that those lessons will be more painful because no one is at the wheel of their relationship. This path tends to meander from difficult experience to difficult experience until we finally wake up and consciously choose to grow through joy instead of pain.

My intention in writing these pages is to encourage, assist and inspire you and your partner to consciously choose the path of joy and to be willing to learn and apply new ways of communicating your deepest thoughts, feelings and dreams to each other in a sacred space of safety and love.

The Quest

The ideas enclosed within are here to assist you in moving your relationship on a direct course toward joy. Like the ancient Greek myth of Jason and the Argonauts and their quest for the Golden Fleece, there will be challenges along the way for you to overcome. However, the quest is well worth it because the Golden Fleece that you are searching for is a passionate, joyful and richly fulfilling shared experience with the person you have chosen to walk through time with, your partner. Let the quest begin!

PART I

Practical Communication Techniques

Chapter 1

Raise the Level of Your Expectations

Nobody succeeds beyond their wildest expectations unless they begin with some wild expectations.

Ralph Charell,
American Author.

Many times in life, we settle for much less than we truly deserve. When it comes to relationships we seem to lower our expectations even more. Somehow, we feel that if we lower our needs and desires within the relationship then we won't be deeply disappointed when those needs aren't realized.

A few generations ago, our ancestors had even lower expectations than we do. For them the most important thing was survival. The man usually desired a loyal woman who could take care of the home and raise his children, and if he was very lucky, he would have sex with his wife more than once a month. The woman usually desired a loyal man who could financially support the family, put out the garbage, and if she were very lucky, she would have sex with her husband less than once a month.

Today, our expectations have changed considerably. We still desire a secure home and family life but we have more sophisticated wants and needs. Some of those desires are the ability to travel, find fulfilling work, create financial freedom and, hopefully, enjoy deep emotional satisfaction in a relationship. At least, this is what we anticipate and eagerly work towards at the beginning of our relationship. Because most of us haven't learned the communication skills necessary to maintain this early momentum of the "honeymoon" in our relationship, the overall level of satisfaction and fulfilment between you and your partner begins to decline over time.

Happily never after

From an early age, films, magazines and television bombard us with images of blissful couples living life to the fullest in the land of "happily ever after." It all looks so easy. By the time we are of marrying age, we have high expectations of having total fulfillment in a relationship. When we are actually in a relationship we quickly discover that the day-to-day reality of life starts chipping away at our dream. A few years into the relationship there's a sharp decline in the overall satisfaction that we receive from the union. For some reason we just accept it, saying, "Oh well, this is exactly what 'they' said would happen. It happens to everybody."

At one time your partner was on the edge of the seat eagerly anticipating your every word. Now you couldn't get their attention with a loudspeaker blaring into their ear. Remember when you used to go dancing together until the early hours of the morning? Now the closest you ever get to the dance floor is watching MTV on a Saturday morning with your kids.

However, "Wait a minute," you say. "So what if we're not going out as much as we used to do? We're adults now and we have responsibilities. There are other pleasures in life like washing the dishes or doing homework with the kids." Or maybe this — "Well just because we can't travel overseas anymore doesn't mean that we can't have fun. We can go to Disney World again. Maybe one day, when we're retired and the children are grown, we can go on a cruise and play senior citizens bridge before our arthritis-easing afternoon nap." Or how about, "We used to look deeply into each other's eyes and whisper sweet words of love but that stopped a long time ago. But that's okay because isn't it natural for romance to die after a few years? We love each other but we're not 'in love' with each other anymore."

This is not a dress rehearsal

When did you buy into the false belief that you would have to postpone your aliveness and your passion for some other time in your life? What makes you so sure you're going to be around for the retirement years?

When did you start settling for less in your relationship? Are you going to just sit back and let your relationship steadily run downhill? Is this as good as it gets? I don't think so!

Happily while together, absolutely!

You have within you the power to completely regenerate your relationship. Whether you're together for the rest of your lives or just the next two years, you can choose to spend that time with your partner enjoying tons more passion, laughter and love than you're settling for now. It only takes knowledge and a mutual affirmative commitment to turn things around.

The very fact that you have purchased this book tells me that you have the determination and courage to build new pathways to fulfillment and to regenerate your original dream.

Raise the bar

Everyone is unique, with different needs, hopes, and desires. Search inside your soul and ask yourself what are my needs; what are my deepest desires for a relationship? What are the qualities that I would like my partner to possess? There isn't a definitive answer that would apply to everyone. What works for me may not necessarily ring your bell. Don't settle for less. Expect the best.

Considering the incredible variety and number of possible

partners you can choose from, why would you want to settle for a partner who doesn't possess the specific qualities you desire? If you're going to exclude all other people from having an intimate relationship with you so that you could spend your time with one person, I trust you chose or will choose well by putting a lot of thought into your needs and desires for a life partner.

> Life is largely a matter of expectation.
> Horace (BC 65-8),
> Italian Poet.

Connect on all levels

Since we exist on four levels, **physical, mental, emotional,** and **spiritual,** I strongly believe your life partner should reflect compatibility on all four levels. In a relationship, it's tough enough under the best conditions to create and maintain a fulfilling partnership even when you have all four levels of compatibility happening with your partner. It's impossible if you don't. If your current relationship is not experiencing a connection on one or more of these levels, it's important to use the tools in this book to re-establish harmony in those missing areas, whether physical, mental, emotional, or spiritual.

If, for some reason, after evaluating your current relationship you cannot regenerate the missing levels because they were never there to begin with, it doesn't mean that you have to abandon your union. Many people choose to remain in a relationship for practical reasons and that is perfectly okay, although you probably won't experience fulfillment with your partner on all possible levels.

Another possibility is that you may strongly desire fulfillment in your relationship, while your partner is neither interested nor willing to work for it. Quite often one partner may appear to be satisfied and content in the relationship while the other wants change and renewal. Even if you both diligently work to revive your relationship, you may discover that no matter how much energy you pour into it, it's impossible to revive or reestablish a strong connection.

You are then faced with two choices. Your first choice is to settle for less, lower your expectations and just grin and bear it for the remainder of your life. Your second choice is to recognize that your time is over as a couple, to dissolve the bonds of your relationship as elegantly as possible, and then to go on your merry individual ways.

Rethink your relationship expectations

It's very important that you take the time to get clear about your needs, desires and expectations within your relationship. I recommend that you write these targets down on paper, as the process of writing will assist you in gaining the clarity and insight needed to know just what it will take for you to be fulfilled in your relationship.

There's no need to put any pressure on yourself to complete a perfect list of expectations right away. Start the process by jotting down as many needs and desires as you can think of right now and as time goes by you can add further expectations to your list. It's a powerful wish list that works.

If both you and your partner are participating in the processes of this book, then it's a good idea for each of you to individually create your own list of expectations for your relationship without consulting the other. After you have finished writing your list, you can then sit down and discuss your expectations with each other. It can be a very revealing experience to see how close or how far you are from each other with your expectations.

You can then hash out, compromise, and ultimately formulate your mutual list of expectations for your relationship. By setting up this agreement of relationship expectations, you put into operation the power of intention, which will greatly assist you in making these expectations a reality for both of you.

> *High expectations
> are the key to everything.*
> Sam Walton (1918-1992),
> American, Founder of Wal-Mart.

In order to get your mental ball rolling, the following is a list of expectations that I aspire to in my relationship. You can use them as a guide to assist you in gaining clarity about your own expectations. For me, though, they are some of the personal goals that I strive for in my relationships.

If you're currently not in a relationship and would like to attract a partner into your life who meets your needs and desires, get out a sheet of paper and start writing.

CAUTION: The following list of expectations is only a possibility. They're targets to shoot for.

Don't compare your current relationship to the following list or you may be disappointed in the comparison. It takes time and effort to bring the reality of these ideas into your relationship as it does any noble quest.

In 1961 when John F Kennedy created an intention and expectation that by 1970 "We choose to go to the moon," it didn't happen overnight. He mobilized the dynamic scientific resources of the most powerful nation on Earth and it still took eight years before his goal was achieved.

In some ways the quest for the moon was a piece of cake compared to manifesting the reality of the following expectations. Yet, it's vital that we shoot for the moon when it comes to our expectations within our most intimate relationship. So here are some suggestions for expectations to target.

A close mental affinity

Expect to:
• Mutually enjoy a compatible mental connection where you can stimulate each other's mind by assisting each other in

seeing things from a different angle.
• Enjoy clear verbal communication with each other and feel safe in sharing your thoughts.
• Share a similar sense of humor.
• Teach as well as learn from each other.
• Respect each other's point of view.
• Enjoy stimulating and humorous conversations with each other.

A close emotional connection

• Experience an emotionally secure relationship where each person takes responsibility for their emotional impact on the other. In other words, if either of you breaks a commitment or hurts each other in any way, then take responsibility for your emotional impact on the other by apologizing and committing to changing the hurtful behavior.
• Receive emotional support from each other in your times of need.
• Have the courage to open your heart fully and to share your deepest feelings, fears and joy in safety and in love.
• Experience ever-increasing feelings of higher emotions such as ecstasy and bliss.
• Fully communicate any feelings of hurt or anger that you may have and not expect the other to read your mind.
• Respect each other's limits or boundaries.
• Argue fairly so that no one gets deeply hurt.
• Share power and control equally in your relationship.
• Have truth as the foundation of your relationship where you both practice complete honesty with each other.
• Experience deep compassion for each other's light and shadow aspects of being.

A strong physical attraction

• Physically enjoy a strong attraction to each other.
• Possess similar needs of affection and touch.
• Have a similar sexual rhythm and desire level.

- Mutually experience radiant health by being responsible with diet and exercise.
- Be physically active together and enjoy the beauty of nature.

A strong spiritual resonance

- Perceive life with a greater vision and value your relationship as a sacred gift.
- Explore higher levels of consciousness using love as the fuel which will take you there.
- Mutually create your own unique spiritual vision so that you can hold the framework of your relationship in a higher view.

Also expect to:
- Enjoy similar interests in life.
- Put each other #1 in life because when you both appreciate each other at that level, the mutual support received uplifts every other area of your life.
- Have a mutually strong commitment to your relationship.
- Share ongoing romantic interludes with each other, surprising and being surprised at every opportunity.
- Have the strength and willingness to work through difficult issues in your union.
- Experience exciting holidays together.
- Enjoy a prosperous life together where over time you work toward creating the financial freedom and security that you have always desired.
- Enjoy spontaneous moments of fun and adventure.
- Share the physical responsibilities of the home such as housework and parenting.
- Respect each other as best friends.
- Know confidently that your relationship can withstand the most intense storms of life, and after the winds recede you will find yourself still standing shoulder to shoulder with hearts fully open.

> It's a funny thing about life: if you refuse to accept anything but the best, you very often get it.
> W. Somerset Maugham (1874-1965),
> British Novelist, Playwright.

I'm sure a part of you may be saying, "Des, you've got to be kidding, not on this planet! This seems impossible."

Maybe you're right; it may be impossible for you. You will never know unless you value your relationship enough to give it a fair go. All I know is that the moon seemed far away at one time and yet you can see moon rocks in museums all over the Earth.

How would you feel if your relationship experienced this level of connection or something greater? What if you just accomplished one important expectation, to learn to argue fairly with each other so as not to cause pain, would it then be worth it to you?

Don't be concerned if you are presently in a relationship that's not anywhere near achieving these previous expectations. From wherever you now find yourself, if you and your partner have a strong intention and commitment to create a relationship that reflects these expectations, I have no doubt that you will get there. All it takes is patience and dedication to achieve positive results.

I won't kid you by saying that it will be easy. In fact, it will be one of the most difficult and yet rewarding experiences of your life to date. For you to get to this level of intimacy, you must look deeper into your heart than ever before and gently uproot the parts of yourself that sabotage your relationship through repressed anger, hurt and fear. You must get past your deep-seated fear of abandonment which holds you back from totally committing to your relationship.

I trust that this book will act as a guide to place you firmly on the only true path of life, the reason we came here to Earth, the path of love.

Chapter 2

Communicate or Disintegrate

> "What we have here... is a failure to communicate!"
>
> Boss man,
> (Film - Cool Hand Luke)

The single biggest problem arising in relationships is the lack of effective communication and understanding between intimate partners.

In my relationship research, it is the number one complaint I hear, day in and day out. For example, someone may say to me, "Every time I bring up an issue she's sensitive to, she blows up and I can't get a word in for the next 20 minutes." Alternatively, "When I confront him with the truth about my feelings, he shuts down by not answering me and just walks away. It infuriates me that he won't respond."

Even with the best of intentions, clear and balanced communication can fly right out the window when emotions are involved. It takes a strong commitment to be fair in your dialogues with your partner, and to overcome the tension that develops between speaking your truth and listening to theirs.

Webster's Dictionary gives this definition of the word: **Communicate: from the Latin word communicare which means to share, impart, partake 1) to make** *known 2) to transmit and receive information 3) to put oneself into close connection or relationship with another 4) participate, share 5) to send information or messages back and forth 6) interchange of thoughts or opinions.*

Think about the last time you and your partner were having a meaningful "communication" in the form of an argument.

Would the definitions for communicate, as described above, apply to your communication? Were you participating and sharing? Were you both in close connection with each other? Did you both transmit and receive information?

Chances are that you both would have come up a little short of honoring the full definitions of the word "communicate". You are not alone. Most couples have difficulty in the communication of their thoughts and feelings to each other.

Are you monologuing or dialoguing?

Webster's Dictionary defines:
Monologue: *a long speech uttered by one person while in the company of others.*
Dialogue: *1) an exchange of ideas and opinions 2) a conversation between two or more persons.*

Looking back on my life, I would have to say that many of my previous communications with former partners were monologues. We both began to speak in a dialogue, which usually degenerated quickly into two monologues.

Desperate to be heard, we were talking at each other, instead of to each other. Quite often, the tone of the monologues would become verbally intense and the volume would increase because we each could see that our message was not getting across.

I can remember those times being very painful because the best intentions were lost in the escalating intensity of the conversation. My desire to be heard often overwhelmed my ability to listen. What good is it if you deliver a perfect monologue when no one is paying attention?

> The way we communicate with others and with ourselves ultimately determines the quality of our lives.
>
> Anthony Robbins, (1960 -),
> Author, speaker, peak performance expert.

In his book *Between People*, John A Sanford likens the process of communication between individuals to tossing a ball back and forth. You throw the ball and I catch it. You speak your message and I receive it. Just as you need another person to play catch with a ball, communication also requires two people who are willing to play.

In order to throw the ball successfully to another, you must toss it with just the right amount of force, directly to the catcher's waiting hands. If you throw the ball inaccurately or with too much force, the person catching will have a hard time holding on to it and will probably drop the ball.

When communicating with another it's important to focus your attention and deliver your words to them in such a way that they will be able to receive your message. If you communicate ineffectively or too forcibly, the person receiving your message will find it hard to listen and will probably reject it. When tossing a ball, a natural rhythm develops where each person alternates between throwing and receiving the ball. It's a natural give and receive process that alternates quickly between the thrower and the catcher. As long as each person participates in the game of toss by throwing and receiving the ball accurately, the game continues.

In a successful dialogue, each person alternates speaking and listening to each other in a natural rhythm and flow. We quickly perceive signals that tell us when to speak and when to listen. If we are fully attentive and engaged in the conversation, a communication is achieved, with each person knowing that the other has successfully received their message. This results in both individuals feeling connected and satisfied.

An unsuccessful dialogue occurs when there is an attempt by either person to dominate the conversation. One way of dominating is not allowing the other to speak. Another way is by refusing to listen. Either way, the natural rhythm of giving and receiving information is disrupted and the communication becomes ineffective. The consequences of disruptive communication are feelings of isolation, disappointment and disconnection.

Blocks to effective communication

Verbal domination is controlling the discussion by means of unfairly taking over the conversation to prevent someone else from speaking. Not equally sharing speaking time breeds frustration in the partner not allowed to speak. Dictators of dialogue are people who want their own way. They won't allow another to speak because they fear sharing power and want to maintain control.

Dictators always look good until the last minutes.
Tomas Masaryk, (1850-1937),
Liberator of Czechoslovakia.

Blame is a word derived from the Greek word blasphemos, which means evil speaking. When you point the finger of blame at your partner by finding fault with them, you automatically put them into a defensive position. When feeling attacked, a natural reaction is to fight back. Accusing your partner is counterproductive to harmonious communication because the nature of blame is inflammatory. Blame is a tactic used to produce guilt and shame in your partner so that they will more readily submit to your will.

When you blame others, you give up your power to change.
Dr Robert Anthony,
American educator.

Excessive anger interferes in the communication process by adding overly aggressive energy to the words being spoken. It usually inflames the situation by escalating the intensity of dialogue. These verbal exchanges can sometimes cause great harm to both of you. Because of excessive anger, you may both have forgotten the original point of the conversation and wind up on a different track altogether. It's impossible to experience balanced communication while rage is being expressed.

> Temper is a weapon that we hold by the blade.
> — Sir James M. Barrie, (1860-1937), British playwright.

Refusing to listen is a control tactic that is a passive way of dominating a conversation by not allowing the speaker's message to enter your mind. If you refuse to hear your partner's message then you won't be influenced by it either.

> It is a rare person who wants to hear what he doesn't want to hear.
> — Dick Cavett, (1936 -), Talk show host, entertainer.

Being right stands in the way of effective communication. It's an overriding need to establish your point of view as the correct and only one. It immediately establishes that you are not open to a dialogue with your partner because you stubbornly resist any new information that may cause you to alter your viewpoint. It's all about control.

> You can be right or you can be happy.
> — Gerald G. Jampolsky, American psychiatrist, lecturer, author.

Deception is extremely toxic to healthy communication within your relationship. It is impossible to have a successful dialogue with your partner if you are lying in any way. Withholding your truth is a defensive measure because you fear the consequences of revealing how you truly feel. Lying only gives you temporary safety. The act of lying immediately erodes the very foundations of trust. Lying is about fear and a lack of courage to speak your truth.

> When a man lies,
> he murders some part of the world.
>
> Merlin.

Disengagement is withdrawing from the communication before it is finished. It prevents resolution and completion of the issue being discussed. Sometimes when your partner says things that upset you, you immediately end the conversation by walking away or saying, "I don't want to talk about this anymore." Disengagement is again about control.

> A coward is one who, in a perilous emergency,
> thinks with his legs.
>
> Ambrose Bierce, (1842-1914),
> Editor, author, journalist.

Interruptions physically prevent you and your partner from communicating with each other by preventing you from focusing on what's being said. It's vital to hold important dialogues at a time when you will not be interrupted by children, television, phone calls or the dog.

> Give whatever you are doing and whoever you are
> with, the gift of your attention.
>
> Jim Rohn,
> American author, speaker, philosopher.

Lack of commitment to the process of working through issues, sharing your truth, and truly wanting to improve the relationship is one of the biggest obstacles to good communication. If the commitment to work toward the goal of increased intimacy in the relationship is not there, then clear communication with your partner will not happen. It takes both of you to be committed to the process of better communication in your relationship for there to be greater understanding between you. If either of you won't commit to putting in the effort, at least have the courage to tell your partner that you are not interested. Then at least you will both have an understanding of where the partnership stands. If one person wants to communicate and the other one doesn't, then you're obviously moving in different directions and it's time to face this truth.

Until one is committed, there is hesitancy, the chance to draw back, always ineffectiveness. Concerning all acts of initiative and creation, there is one elementary truth the ignorance of which kills countless ideas and splendid plans: that the moment one definitely commits oneself, then providence moves too. All sorts of things occur to help one that would never otherwise have occurred. A whole stream of events issues from the decision, raising in one's favor all manner of unforeseen incidents, meetings and material assistance which no man could have dreamed would have come his way. Whatever you can do or dream you can, begin it. Boldness has genius, power and magic in it. Begin it now.

Johann Von Goethe, (1749-1832),
German novelist, poet.

The Power of Commitment

The ideas in this book won't fully work unless you and your partner have the intention and desire to learn and apply these concepts in your daily life. Ideally, it's best if you commit to the process of communicating more truthfully in your relationship. Above all, you both must agree to play fair because the only referee in this important game of love is you and your commitment to growth, both personally and in your union together.

Otherwise, you may as well put this book down and wait for the slow, inevitable decline in the quality of your relationship. On the other hand, you could regenerate your union by energetically learning and applying new communications skills, and risk venturing into the new unexplored territory of your mutual unexpressed truth. This sharing of truth could open you to the possibility of moving into the land of passion, ecstasy and a fullness of heart that you have desired in your dreams.

The power of the written word

The process of committing your name to paper solidifies your mental agreement and brings into action the power of intention.

By creating a focused intention, you combine the resources of your will and desire to assist you in creating successful results. In the course of this book you will be called upon to sign various agreements which will reinforce your commitment to improving the communication process in your relationship.

Please deeply consider the meaning of these agreements before signing your name.

By signing these agreements you're not saying that you will perfectly abide by them. What you are saying is that you are intending to keep your commitments to the best of your ability, and that sometimes you may falter. If you do fall down, you just pick yourself up, accept the responsibility for your stumble, and prepare to give it another go.

These agreements are designed for couples who are ready and committed to the process of improving their communication skills. If you are single, or your partner is not willing to participate in these agreements, it's perfectly okay to sign them on your own. You will still grow by discovering dynamic new pathways of communication.

Maybe your partner feels that there isn't a need to

improve communications within your relationship. Perhaps they're not willing or ready to sign any agreements. It doesn't necessarily mean that the communication level of the relationship cannot be improved. It may just take a while longer. Sometimes, if you alone commit to improving your communications skills, your partner will be inspired to grow along with you. If your partner does not feel ready to sign at this time, then don't despair because they may agree to join you at some future date. Whatever you do, don't pressure your partner to participate if he or she is reluctant to do so.

Perhaps you're the one that has resistance to signing these agreements. If you sign documents such as a bank loan, marriage license, tax form, or personal bank check, why should you refuse to voluntarily sign an agreement between you and your partner to improve the quality of your relationship? The only possible deeper reason would be your reluctance to change your methods of communication. Look within to see if your resistance is because of your own refusal to communicate fairly within your relationship. These agreements should not be taken lightly as they are a reflection of the integrity of your word.

What follows is a written agreement to be signed by you alone or you and your partner which will assist in fully committing to the process of clear and effective communication in your relationship. Please fill in your names and okay the agreement with your signatures before proceeding further in the book. By signing this agreement you are signaling each other that you are truly committed to improving the quality of your communication within your relationship.

Fair Communication Agreement

As intimate partners,

We_____

and_____ **agree to earnestly commit:**

- to be willing to learn effective ways of communicating with each other,
- to participate in using the techniques within this book for a minimum of 90 days,
- to give our best efforts to improve the overall quality of our relationship.

_____   _____
          Partner   Partner
Signatures

_____   _____
           Date   Date

Chapter 3

The Gift of Listening

Nature gave us one tongue and two ears so we could hear twice as much as we speak.
>
> Epictetus, (50-120 BCE),
> Stoic Philosopher.

The roots of unclear communication can be traced back to one main source — poorly developed listening skills.

In our youth, listening to others was often an unpleasant experience, because adults forced us to pay attention to their messages while refusing to listen to ours. No one taught us how to listen effectively to another person in a balanced dialogue, where each person would alternate speaking and listening.

There are good reasons for your resistance to listening to others. The roots of your resistance can be traced back to your family of origin and early school environment.

"Listen to me...I'm talking to you!"

How does that make you feel? It certainly doesn't create a desire to enthusiastically lend me your ear, does it? That's because you cannot demand attention from another human being. Our attention can only be given as a gift.

Remember the feeling that came over you as a young child when your parents might have said these same words? You may have given the appearance that you were listening, by looking directly at them, but you probably were not listening. In fact, you were probably angry that another big person was telling you to do something that you really were not interested in doing.

Children should be seen and not heard

As children, when we had something to say often no one was willing to listen. Listening to others or getting them to listen to us was about as much fun as cleaning out the cat litter box. From an early age, you were taught that it was very important for you to listen to what your parents had to say or there could be very serious consequences. In fact, what you were actually listening to was a lecture, as it certainly wasn't a give-and-take communication with your parents. Then other authority figures, such as your grandparents, older siblings, and teachers started demanding that you listen to them as well.

Consider the fact that a child usually attends years of primary education where they are forced to sit still and listen to the teacher speak for about six hours a day. It goes without saying that the child is not allowed to speak. In other words, unless answering a question, the child is not learning how to communicate in a two-way process but is being taught to listen to lectures. To the child who is only receiving information and not sending any, listening becomes a one-way street of no return.

In two primary areas of early influence, home and school, you were being conditioned to perceive listening as a negative experience. You were being coerced into listening to your parents telling you to do things that you didn't want to do, and in school to listen to your teachers instruct you in subjects that you didn't want to learn. To top it all off, no one was interested in listening to anything that you had to say. It's no wonder that you have an aversion to listening to others!

How many times do I have to tell you?"

You quickly learned coping mechanisms to deal with all

that unwanted information that bombarded your eardrums. Your main course of action was the "tune them right out" strategy. It was especially effective with the "look them straight in the eye" tactic, which gave the illusion that you were totally paying attention to their rantings.

Later, if you were ever confronted about your failure to remember, denial was always a lifesaver.

"Beau, do you remember me telling you last week to clean your room?"

"No dad, I don't remember you saying anything to me."

"What do you mean you don't remember? You were looking right at me and nodding your head!"

"But dad I wasn't nodding a yes. I was just watching Kylie jump up and down on the bed!"

Does this sound familiar to you? You probably remember doing something like this to your parents or you have children of your own who are running this game on you on a regular basis.

By the time you become an adult, you are a master at the tune them right out strategy of listening. You can't help it; it's an automatic reflex action. It comes from a lifetime of not listening to others. Don't take this personally. It's an affliction which affects all people from all cultures. We all could learn to sharpen our listening skills.

Listening opens the doors of the heart

The main ingredients in good listening are giving the gift of your attention, and seeking to understand another. One of the major stumbling blocks of communication comes from one individual frantically wanting to be heard without paying attention to what the other person has just said.

It's ironic how in conversation we demand the attention of another and yet we have difficulty listening to them. We insist on getting something that we are not willing to give. It all boils down to verbal selfishness. We like to talk and have others listen to us but when it comes to returning the favor, we get greedy.

Are you a conversation hog?

Do you or your partner have a large appetite for speaking and a small appetite for listening? If you're like most of us, you would probably have to answer this question in the affirmative. Dominating conversations by speaking your truth without listening to theirs is a selfish act anyway you look at it.

Speaking with a verbal bully is a disempowering experience. Quite often, you will leave the dialogue feeling shamed, as if your point of view didn't deserve to be expressed. Another emotion you will often feel is anger. This anger may be directed toward yourself for not having the courage to speak your truth, or toward your partner for shutting you down.

> I feel that if a person has problems communicating the very least he can do is to shut up.
> Tom Lehrer, (1928 -),
> American musician, song writer.

Let's not get too judgmental here; we have all dominated a conversation at one time or another in our lives. It's about honestly looking within, uncovering our tendencies to control, and learning to verbally play fair and share power in our communications with others.

Verbal dominance is not an unusual occurrence and it occurs all over the world. If you want to have true communication in your relationship then you must decide to share the floor equally.

Put your heart back in your hearing

Listening to another's deepest feelings is like merging with the beat of their heart. It is an amazing gift to be able to listen patiently to your partner's stories. It's worth every effort that you can make to refine your listening skills.

Effective dialogue has its roots in a balance of speaking

and listening. Generosity and fair play are essential ingredients in successful communication. Treating your partner with respect by giving them the gift of your ear will encourage your partner to return the favor to you.

It's a good feeling when you know that someone is listening attentively to the message you are speaking. The gift of their listening makes you feel valued. You know that they are interested in what you have to say and it makes you more inclined to want to listen to their story. That's when the magic of communication takes place.

I didn't quite get that

When it comes to language, we all have different meanings and understandings of words used in a conversation. Take the word "power," for example. For one partner it may mean energy and the ability to get things accomplished while for the other partner power could represent domination and suppression.

Because we have different understandings of words, the art of communication can often be inaccurate, even with the best intentions and under favorable circumstances. If we are not carefully listening to the deeper meaning of what another is trying to communicate, then it becomes impossible to understand their message.

So, when you are listening to somebody, completely, attentively, then you are listening not only to the words, but also to the feeling of what is being conveyed, to the whole of it, not part of it.

Jiddu Krishnamurti, (1895-1986),
Indian theosophist.

Words and language not only represent thoughts and ideas but also embody feelings. In a dialogue with another, it's important to listen to the underlying feelings that are being conveyed in the communication. It's usually the deeper vulnerable feelings that are the most difficult to communicate. You are able to create a sense of security for your partner by listening patiently to their message.

When your partner truly feels that you are listening without judgment, long-held emotions can be expressed, safely released, and a true communication can occur.

The vulnerability of many of your feelings, and a reluctance to reveal them to your partner, necessitates the importance of discovering new ways where you can communicate securely with each other. One way is by using the technique of dynamic listening.

Dynamic Listening is a combination of both passive and active listening.
• To listen passively is to pay close attention to your partner's message and receive it.
• To listen actively is to be able to reflect back to the sender of the message an accurate account of what you just heard.

Dynamic Listening consists of three parts:
> **Listening without interruption** – allows the necessary speaking time to your partner to clearly communicate their message to you. By opening your ears and closing your mouth, you are able to fully hear and comprehend what they are saying.
> **Summarize and mirror** – the message back to the person speaking. Recap or paraphrase what you heard and reflect it back to the sender. Giving feedback signals your partner that you were paying attention and have received their communication accurately. This encourages them to keep sending their message to you.
> **Equal speaking time** – gives both of you a fair amount of time in which to speak your truth and listen to your partner's truth. Sharing speaking time is a healthy sign of mutual respect for each other and your relationship.

Sounds good on paper, but how do you do it in a real life?

Initially, the concept of Dynamic Listening is not easy to achieve because of our resistance to listening. With practice and a mutual dedication to learning a more effective way of listening, it gets easier over time.

There is a potent communication tool which will put you on the fast track to successful communication in your relationship. It was passed down from a people with one of the ancient spiritual traditions of the earth, the Native Americans.

To assist you in putting these concepts of listening into action, and to create a sacred space where you and your partner can communicate your deepest feelings and truth to each other in safety, the next chapter of this book will reveal the power of **The Talking Stick.**

Chapter 4

The Talking Stick

Communication is a skill that you can learn. It's like riding a bicycle or typing. If you're willing to work at it, you can rapidly improve the quality of every part of your life.

Brian Tracy (1944-),
American author, trainer, businessman.

The Talking Stick is a powerful tool which will revolutionize the quality of communication in your relationship. Using the Talking Stick allows you the safety to talk about the most sensitive issues confronting you within your union. It teaches you to respect the viewpoints of your partner, while still granting you the privilege to disagree.

Native Americans used the Talking Stick as a way to let everyone speak their truth within a council or tribal meeting. It was used for centuries by many tribes in North America. It provided a means by which each individual in the tribe could speak to the other members of the tribe without interruption. When in a council, whoever held the stick also held the undivided attention of the tribe.

After the individual spoke her truth, she passed the Talking Stick to the next person who wanted to speak. After all the members of the tribe who wanted to talk had spoken, the tribal elder or chief would make a decision, considering all the viewpoints that were heard. It was a fair and democratic form of communication. Everyone listened attentively to the tribal speakers and contributed to the discussion.

Sometimes a different object was used other, such as a peace pipe, crystal or feather. Whatever the object used, it symbolized the power and liberty for a person to speak deeply from the heart without any fear of punishment or disgrace. The design of the Talking Stick always reflected the individual tastes and style of the person crafting it. First, the tribal members would find a stick by walking in the forest and choosing a piece of wood that they were drawn toward. The Native Americans had a profound respect for nature and approached the assembly of the Talking Stick with a sense of ritual and reverence. Often an eagle feather would be attached, symbolizing the courage to speak with wisdom and truth. A stone or crystal would sometimes be added to the stick, along with a piece of fur.

The Talking Stick then possessed representations of the four kingdoms of life on Earth. The stick symbolized the plant kingdom, the crystal corresponded to the mineral realm, the piece of fur and feather stood for the animal kingdom and finally the person holding the stick completed the circle by representing the human element.

Sticks as symbols of power

Throughout history, pieces of wood in the form of a stick or a pole have been used as a symbol of power in all cultures of the world. The magic wand of the magician, the staff of religious leaders, the gavel in court and the scepter of royalty have all been used as symbols of authority. Whoever held a "stick of power" also held the power of speech. Their word was law.

Talking tool for today

The concept of the Talking Stick is still very relevant in our modern times because it provides us with a formal procedure of communication that teaches us how to listen effectively to another. When holding the Talking Stick, we also feel encouraged to speak our truth in safety.

The Talking Stick is particularly handy when having conversations that are sensitive or emotional in nature. When our partner tells us something that we don't like, we usually have an emotional reaction to what was said and the conversation can quickly change into a confrontation.

Create your own Talking Stick

A Talking Stick can be made just about any way you would like. Go into your backyard or take a walk in the woods and find a piece of wood or a stick that can be held in one hand. (A stick under twelve inches would be about right.) Try to involve your partner and search for the stick together, since the process of using the Talking Stick will involve both of you.

You can dress up the Talking Stick any way you like by attaching a semi-precious stone, feather or any object that has meaning to you. Just follow your creativity and construct the Talking Stick in whatever way you prefer. You may even choose to leave it totally plain. It's not the design of the stick which is important but the significance and meaning that you attach to it which is the key.

In the past, when I had misplaced my Talking Stick, I often grabbed a writing pen, piece of rock or whatever I could find to serve as a designated Talking Stick.

Over time, I created a method of using the Talking Stick that adapted the Native American tradition to a more contemporary style in order to make it more user-friendly.

Learning to use the Talking Stick

Today's fast-moving world culture has caused me to modify the way in which the Talking Stick is used. In our day-to-day conversations, we speak rapidly and have a much shorter attention span than the early users of the Talking Stick. Because of this, it's important for each person holding the Talking Stick to speak in short periods of no more than 20 seconds, or the person listening will not remember and retain the message.

I've developed two basic methods for using the Talking Stick. Each method has distinct benefits over the other. (**Method 2** is located in the appendix at the back of this book and is only recommended after becoming fully experienced with **Method 1**)

Method 1 is used to prevent strong emotions from interfering in the communication process. This method is also effective when you do not have a lot of time and you need to work through an issue quickly. It also teaches you how to dialogue with fairness. By using this method, you quickly learn the skills of **Dynamic Listening.**

Here we have **Partner A** and **Partner B:**

Step 1: Partner A speaks first.
• **Partner A** holds the Talking Stick and speaks for a maximum of 20 seconds.
• **Partner B** listens attentively while not interrupting.

Step 2: Partner B summarizes and mirrors what was said back to Partner A.
• **Partner A** releases the Talking Stick by putting it on the table after speaking for a maximum of 20 seconds. This indicates to the listening partner that **Partner A** is finished speaking.
• **Partner B** summarizes or paraphrases what was heard and mirrors it back to **Partner A**, and then asks for confirmation by saying, "Is that right?" (The reason for this is to determine if Partner B correctly heard what **Partner A** said.)
• **Partner A** answers the question, "Is that right?" in one of two ways:
    (1) If **Partner A** says, "Yes that's right," then it becomes **Partner B's** turn to hold the Talking Stick and speak.
    (2) If **Partner A** says, "No that's not what I said," then **Partner A** again picks up the Talking Stick and verbally repeats and clarifies what was originally said. After **Partner B** gets the message correct, it's their turn to speak.

Step 3: Partner B now picks up the Talking Stick and switches roles with Partner A by repeating Steps 1 and 2. Each continues to alternate between speaking and listening until both partners are finished.

(Video Example at www.DesCoroy.com)

Important points to remember

Purpose – The purpose of using the Talking Stick is to provide you and your partner with a safe way of resolving issues of importance by dramatically improving the level of dialogue truly heard by each of you within your relationship.

Commitment – The Talking Stick will support you in improving verbal exchanges within your relationship only to the extent that you have an intention and desire to do so. For it to work, you both must be committed to the process of enhancing your individual communication skills. Usually one partner is initially more committed than the other, so don't be discouraged if one of you is not as enthusiastic about learning a new way of relating. It's important to let your partner know that improving the communication level between you is an essential need that demands to be filled.

If your desire for better communication within your relationship is unwavering and there is a genuine foundation of love between you, then remain steadfast and your partner will almost certainly come around. If not, then your partner's refusal to participate is a major warning sign for danger ahead in your relationship.

Practice – Using the Talking Stick may feel a little bit awkward at the beginning because you're not familiar with this new method of communicating. Be patient. After a while a natural rhythm develops and you will begin to see positive results in the way you and your partner communicate.

Begin it – It only takes one person to call a Talking Stick session if that partner feels there is something important to say. If the partner calling for this session wants to do it right away, then it's important for the other partner to agree to a dialogue as soon as possible. The only reasons not to have an immediate Talking Stick session are if the circumstances don't allow it, or if either one of you is excessively angry.

Timeout – It's okay to communicate while you have some anger running between you but extreme anger will interfere in the dialogue. If the dialogue becomes excessively heated then it's important to call a timeout. A timeout can be a period where you walk away from each other, giving you both a chance to cool down and return to the dialogue when you both feel more balanced.

Don't interrupt – It's essential to remember not to interrupt the other when they are holding the Talking Stick. When your partner holds the Talking Stick, they hold the power of speech and it's important for you to give them your respect by maintaining silence.

The first duty of love is to listen.

Paul Tillich, (1886-1965),
German Protestant theologian, philosopher.

Recap – To summarize or paraphrase the message received from your partner means you take the essence of what was said and feed it back to them by giving your interpretation of what you heard. At first, this may feel a bit mechanical and unusual but keep at it and it will begin to feel very natural.

For example:
Message sent: The wife holds the Talking Stick saying, "When I came home last night, the house was a mess. The kids weren't in bed and the kitchen looked like a pig pen! You

promised me that the kids would be in bed and that you would cook a meal for me."

Message reflected: The husband summarizes what he heard and mirrors it back to the wife, saying "You were very disappointed that I didn't keep my promise to prepare a meal for you and keep the house in order. You were also upset that the kids were still awake and that the kitchen was trashed. Is that right?"

Listening – Listening to your partner's message and reflecting it back to them does not necessarily mean you agree with it. We often resist listening to others because we sometimes think that if we listen to their viewpoint, we may be persuaded to concur with them. Sure, that's a possibility, and it's also a possibility that you could do the persuading.

Listening means listening and it doesn't necessarily mean agreement. It just means you have received the message, understand what was said and will give it your consideration. Listening also means paying attention to the feelings being conveyed by your partner and not just the words being spoken.

Feedback – The key to the successful use of the Talking Stick is the feedback step, when you mirror back to your partner what was just said to you. It proves to your partner that you have heard the message even though you may disagree with it. There is something very healing and magical about knowing that your partner has fully heard what you said; it creates a potential for greater understanding within the relationship.

Compromise – When extreme differences of view arise between you, the Talking Stick is a perfect tool for creating a bridge of compromise. We can't always have our way in relationships. Negotiate your differences by making concessions to each other on non-vital points because it is essential to creating harmony between you. It takes a mature individual to compromise and by doing so you will gain your partner's respect over time. Compromise is a gift of love.

Resolution – Resolving issues with the Talking Stick is not always possible every time you complete a dialogue. Often a resolution won't take place until after you have digested each other's messages and reconsidered your positions. Quite often you may end a Talking Stick session with opposite points of view. In fact, you may be even more entrenched in your position because you didn't like what the other had just said. However, after a short time of considering what you heard, frequently you are more willing to compromise on your previously fixed positions.

If you are expecting to resolve your differences every time you use the Talking Stick, you will be disappointed.

"For the 37th time, you don't seem to understand that I want to watch the football game," he says as he passes her the Talking Stick. "For the 38th time, you don't realize I don't give a damn about your football game and that I want to go to dinner," she says emphatically.

Be willing to put down the Talking Stick if you're both at an impasse and take the time to consider your partner's view. People dislike changing their mind or being wrong. However, I've often said that no matter how strongly I might hold a point of view, if someone can supply me with new information then I would be willing to consider it and alter my view if it makes sense. It's the reasonable thing to do.

Using the Talking Stick today

The Talking Stick acts as a very effective communication tool by allowing you and your partner enough time to speak to each other uninterrupted. It also encourages the person listening to remember what is being said.

The Talking Stick will prevent your conversations from increasing in emotional intensity by slowing down the speed at which you talk and lowering the volume on anger. By reducing anger, your ability to listen to each other's message will improve. By using the Talking Stick, you will discover how to work through any disagreements. The level of tension between you and your partner will also be greatly reduced. Using the Talking Stick will shore up the foundation of your relationship by giving you a way to communicate more effectively in your union.

In my experience, when the Talking Stick is used in dialogue, an atmosphere of civility and integrity is evoked. It acts as a third party, a fair witness which silently facilitates clearer communication between partners.

Another problem that often arises between couples is when one partner dominates the conversation while the more verbally passive partner says nothing. Usually the passive partner doesn't feel safe enough to speak their truth and the Talking Stick encourages them to be more verbally responsive. It also teaches the verbally dominant partner how to develop the necessary patience to allow their partner to speak.

The Talking Stick saves counseling costs

A professional relationship counselor is actually a Talking Stick who talks. One of the main goals of a counselor is to assist a couple in learning how to communicate more fairly with each other. During most of the time in a counseling session the counselor acts as a referee between a couple by determining who talks and who listens.

Effective use of a Talking Stick can serve the same purpose as a counselor by acting as a symbol of fair and equal communication within your relationship. Sometimes it's absolutely necessary and supportive for a couple to attend counseling sessions but many times it can be sidestepped by simply learning to communicate fairly and more effectively with each other.

By communicating your differences with the safety of the Talking Stick, you will prevent the buildup of resentments, which could cause a more serious collapse in your relationship down the road. The frequent use of the Talking Stick will assist you and your partner in clearing out stagnant emotions that have been blocking the path to increased passion and harmony in your relationship.

The Talking Stick is a way for you and your partner to really learn the skills of Active Listening, and after a while you may find that you can have meaningful communication with your partner in which each person listens and reflects back to each other fairly without needing the safety of the Talking Stick.

Chapter 5

Truth, the Lifeblood of Love

The truth will set you free, but first it will piss you off.

Mal Pancoast.

Let's begin this chapter by speaking some truth: We have all lied at some point in our lives. In fact, the great majority of us continue to lie on a regular basis. We can call them white lies, minor deceptions or giant whoppers; whatever, they are still lies.

We live in a world where lying is the norm and truth is often the exception. Compared to the animal world, we humans come up a bit short in the honesty department. When a dog is angry with you, I can't imagine him choosing to lie by hiding his anger with a wag of his tail and sitting down to extend his front paw in friendship. With animals, what you see is what you get. It's all body language with them.

Unlike animals, humans use language as the primary form of communication. We pay much more attention to words then we do to body language. Because of our reliance on spoken language, if we choose to deceive another it's easy to do so —we just rearrange the words to distort the truth. Over the years, we've become very sophisticated at it.

Lies are verbal illusions of events that did not take place

From the time that we can speak, we quickly learn that twisting the truth can prevent us from getting into trouble with our parents. Those same parents constantly told us to tell the truth and then, by their example, taught us to do the exact opposite. It's very confusing for a young child to see a parent tell his boss on the phone that he can't go to work that day because he's unwell, and later watch his father throw the fishing rod into the car for a day at the lake.

It's no wonder that by the time we are adults we have mastered the art of bending the truth. We don't give ourselves too much grief by feeling excessively guilty about it because everyone does it.

Just because it's the norm does not mean it's right. I wouldn't take too much comfort in the fact that "everyone does it" because at one time "everyone" spent Sunday afternoons in the Roman Coliseum watching gladiators being ripped to shreds by wild animals.

> Always tell the truth - it's the easiest thing to remember.
> David Mamet, (1947 -),
> American playwright.

By the time we are ready for intimate relationships, we are well trained in the art of deception. This inclination for twisting the truth will cause irreparable harm in your partnerships. In relationships, there is no such thing as a small white lie because every deceit works against the building of trust within the union.

We assume that the individual we can trust the most is the person who is at our side, sharing an intimate relationship. However, if you lie to each other, ultimately you'll weaken faith.

If you can't trust the person you're sleeping with, then who the hell can you trust?

The Power of the Word

Fundamentally, human beings are molded in integrity. Every time we lie, we chip away a portion of our self-esteem and our sense of well-being. When we lie, we immediately feel a sense of shame and regret, which negatively affects our overall self-worth. This lowered self-esteem makes it difficult for us to accept and love ourselves because we always know that we have been deceptive. If we can't love ourselves then it will be impossible to fully love another.

When we speak the truth, the thought in our mind corresponds to the spoken words chosen to represent that thought. Our words will then vibrate with power because the words match the thought.

> Truth is exact correspondence with reality.
> Paramahansa Yogananda,
> Spiritual author, lecturer.

When we choose to lie, the thought in our mind does not match the spoken word. In other words, we consciously misrepresent reality by substituting words that are false.

This counterfeit reality causes our words to lose power because of the disconnection between the thought and the words.

My personal experience has shown me how incredibly destructive lying can be to the structure of relationships. I never imagined I would write about the importance of telling the truth within a relationship, because in the early part of my life I lied so much that I began to believe my own lies. Yet we all have the power to change our behavior if we choose, and that's exactly what I did.

> He who permits himself to tell a lie once, finds it much easier to do it a second and a third time till at length it becomes habitual.
> Thomas Jefferson, (1743 – 1826),
> Third President of the USA.

The lies I told created untold damage to my relationships and often deeply hurt the one I loved. Back then I remember feeling shame and a lack of respect for myself when I lied. Because of the pain I caused to others and myself, I made a fundamental choice to shift away from deception and to move toward the truth. Long-ingrained habits take time to shift but eventually I learned the power of speaking the truth. My relationships are now strengthened by the truth and are supported by a foundation of trust.

Lying destroys relationships

Deception, either as a conscious withholding of information, or purposefully misleading your partner by outright lying, rips apart the bonds of trust within your relationship.

Sometimes your lie may appear to be successful because your partner never finds out the truth. You may feel that you got away with it. In actuality, you never get away with it because even though your partner may not be aware of the truth, you are. Your knowledge of the actual truth will stand in the way of being able to communicate clearly with your partner. It may not happen at first, but as the lies accumulate, so does the resulting friction.

This friction interferes with the intimacy of your relationship. It's extremely difficult to build understanding and trust in your relationship when one or both of you continues to deceive each other in your everyday conversations.

Lies are viruses of love

If you lie about the little things to your partner, you will lie about the bigger things. Many of us are concerned about our partner deceiving us by having a sexual affair outside our relationship, yet we pay little attention to the daily deceptions that we swap with our partner. These "little" deceptions are the real culprits in the destruction of your relationship, energetically dissolving the glue of trust which holds your relationship together.

An affair is usually the last step in the process of emotional withdrawal from a relationship. The only reason it gets to that point is because the attraction levels have been greatly reduced within the relationship. When we withhold our feelings from our partner, the level of passion quickly subsides and we start retreating emotionally. If the lies continue, we eventually get to the point where the person who was once our most trusted confidante becomes the one we now trust the least, as the divorce courts continue to reaffirm on a daily basis.

Truth check

By this time you're probably saying, "But I don't lie that much. Maybe the occasional itsy, bitsy, teeny, little white lie or fib, but that's about as far as it goes." Maybe you're right and it's not a problem for you.

Just to make sure, here's a challenge for you: Starting today and continuing for one week, become aware of how often you "misspeak the truth," or to put it more bluntly, lie. To assist you in becoming conscious of your lies, I suggest you put a rubber band around your left wrist and keep it on for the whole week. Every time you stretch the truth by lying, lightly stretch the rubber band and let it slap you on the wrist.

The reason for this is to give yourself a physical sensation which reaffirms your verbal indiscretion. After a few days, I'm sure you'll be surprised at the amount of times you tweak that rubber band.

Ways we lie:

Lie by exaggeration – is a form of lie where you may overstate a fact that is true by adding information that is not accurate in order to dramatize a point.

For example:
- **Fact** – A man has his first date with a woman. He has seduction on his mind as he takes her back to her place. He finally kisses her on the balcony and as he does he slips backwards and the young lady falls on him, hurting his head. His head is severely bruised so they go to the

emergency room and are up all night waiting for the doctor.
- **Lie by exaggeration** – The next week his best friend asks him, "How did your date go?" and he answers, "Man, it was incredible! She took me back to her place and before you know it, she was all over me. One thing led to another and what do you know, we were up all night."

White lie – is where the only reason you lie is to protect someone from getting hurt, because if you express how you really feel they may react with anger or disappointment.

For example:
- **Fact** – Your wife has just purchased a new dress and after seeing her model it, you think it makes her look like a pear.
- **Fib or white lie** – When your wife asks for your opinion on her dress and you say, "The dress looks quite attractive on you. It accents your curves."

Deliberate lie – is when there is an unmistakable absence of the truth. It's a deliberate attempt to mislead others.

For example:
- **Fact** – You spontaneously decide on the way home from work to have a few drinks with the girls, and you arrive home two hours late.
- **Deliberate lie** – Your husband angrily greets you at the front door wanting to know your whereabouts and you declare, "I'm sorry dear, but I was at the office working on a project that's due tomorrow and I guess I got carried away."

The purpose of this exercise is for you to become aware of how often you may be deceiving yourself and others. If you find you have a habit of not telling the truth then please be gentle with yourself. Don't judge yourself too harshly because lying is a common habit in our culture.

If you don't like the results of your experiment, you have

the power to change the way you communicate. Just begin to speak to others with more accuracy and truth. A new habit takes time to learn so be patient. It's not about being perfect and never telling a lie. It's about striving to express truth in your conversations with a strong commitment to move away from the path of deception. In time, your words will gain power because of the added fuel of truth and your self-esteem will be increasingly enriched.

When you learn to speak the truth, it positively impacts every area of your life. Your words gain power because of the harmonization of your thoughts and speech. Because it's so rare on this planet for a person to consistently speak the truth, you will stand out in the crowd and people will sense that they can trust you. They will be instinctively attracted to you and will offer you their unsolicited support.

The law of attraction states that "like attracts like." If you lie to others, you will attract people into your life who will deceive you. If you consistently speak the truth, you'll attract individuals who are honest and will respond to you in truth.

Open the floodgates of truth with care

You may be tempted to reveal past deceptions to your partner all at once. If you and your partner are not accustomed to telling each other the complete truth, then I would caution you about wanting to fully come clean and immediately confessing your sins. Too much truth at one time can be a hard pill to swallow. As you slowly build trust, you will naturally and intuitively know the best time for revealing your former transgressions. As difficult as it may be to tell your partner the truth, the rewards of doing so will far outweigh the temporary pain of your revelations.

The Talking Stick serves as the perfect instrument for assisting you to speak your truth in safety. It is especially helpful when you are clearing up past deceptions that are sensitive in nature. Of course, the Talking Stick can only work if you're being truthful with each other.

When you shed the excess burden of the past you have been withholding from your partner, you will experience a wonderful sense of freedom and lightness of being. Keep clearing emotional issues with your partner by continuing to share your feelings and thoughts about issues which are important to you. Eventually you'll come to a place where you aren't withholding any stored or repressed feelings and you will begin to experience more joy and passion in your relationship.

Truth builds bridges of trust

Speaking the truth is essential when communicating with your partner. By grounding your relationship in truthfulness, you establish a strong foundation, which can withstand any of the storms of life that may assault your partnership.

> It's essential to tell the truth at all times. This will reduce life's pain. Lying distorts reality. All forms of distorted thinking must be corrected.
> John Bradshaw,
> American author, lecturer, leading expert,
> recovery & dysfunctional families.

When you can count on your partner to tell you the truth, no matter what happens, you will discover new levels of trust you didn't think were possible. These new levels of trust create a sanctuary within your relationship where you will realize deeper levels of emotional safety with each other.

> Truth builds a bridge that spans the space between your hearts.
> Des Coroy

As you mutually reveal more and more of your personal truth, your relationship will enter a deeply rewarding phase of intimacy. Your united courage to stand emotionally naked in each other's presence will put you firmly on the path of trust.

Chapter 6

Entering the War Zone

For every minute you are angry you lose sixty seconds of happiness.
                      Ralph Waldo Emerson, (1803-1882,
                      American poet, essayist.

It seems like a cruel twist of nature. The person you are closest to in life is usually the person who angers you the most. Why is this so? Perhaps because you feel safe enough with the people you love to reveal and express aspects of yourself such as anger or vulnerability that you would never disclose to your acquaintances.

I know from my own experience that learning to accept anger and utilize its positive aspects has been an especially challenging task. For many years, I denied that I even had anger, though it was hard to deny my periodic eruptions of rage as being a problem that was outside of me. My pattern was to deny my anger until the point of explosion when I said things that hurt the people I loved. After seeing the hurtful impact of my anger, I would swing into feelings of shame because of the damage I caused. Each time, I judged my anger as being negative and destructive. I tried to control it by suppressing it again and off I went into a new cycle of suppress, explode, shame and suppress again.

Eventually I stopped blaming others and started looking at my own responsibility for my anger. As I learned to accept my anger and started seeing some of the positive aspects of it, anger ceased being the problem it once was in my life. Not that I don't have the occasional strong feelings of anger, but I'm a saint compared to the angry young man who used to walk around with a chip on his shoulder the size of a watermelon.

One of my favorite statements was: "You're making me angry." In truth, no one can make us angry because we are in control of our reactions to what another says. When I blamed others for my anger, I was playing a victim. In essence, I was telling them that their power to make me angry was greater than my self-control. As long as I blamed my partner, I avoided taking any responsibility for my own anger. Choosing not to react to someone's words or actions by losing control of my anger puts me in the driver's seat by reclaiming my power. We can't control what another will say or do but we have absolute control over our own reactions.

> Anger is a great force. If you control it, it can be transmuted into a power which can move the whole world.
>
> Sri Swami Sivananda, (1887- 1963),
> Indian physician, sage.

Anger often gets a bad rap in our "civilized" world culture. You are taught from an early age that it's not "nice" to be angry with anyone, at any time or for any reason. Nothing could be further from the truth.

Anger is a natural emotion which helps you protect yourself in times of physical or emotional danger. Like an animal that growls when threatened, your anger alerts you and provides dynamic energy which can be used as a shield to an impending threat to your well-being.

If you were taught to trust your anger as the alarm system it truly is, you would be able to safeguard yourself by expressing your anger in a way that would not cause damage to others. The more you trust your anger, the more you're able to respond to any harmful situation with just the right amount of appropriate force.

Resentments are emotional weapons of mass destruction

Because of the cultural suppression of anger, most of the anger you see expressed is usually over the top and especially intense. No wonder you perceive anger as being negative when most of your experience of it has been destructive. It's not the clear, spontaneous expression of anger which hurts others, but the smoldering repressed resentments that build up to the point of explosion which do the most damage.

Anger, excessively expressed or totally repressed, is often the major cause of pain within a relationship. When the pressures of life impinge upon a couple, frustration and anger often arise at the most inopportune moments. If you don't have the necessary skills to safely handle your own or your partner's anger, then it's probably inevitable that anger will do irreparable harm to your relationship.

Learning to accept and heal your anger is a process that will take time. It is beyond the scope of this book to teach you how to effectively handle your anger but I can point you in the right direction. There are many helpful books on the market that can assist you in accepting and expressing your anger safely. One of my favorites is a practical and enlightening book called *Managing Anger* by Gael Lindenfield. If you need further support, then I recommend finding a professional counselor who specializes in healing anger issues.

For the purposes of this book, we will focus on developing skills which will assist you and your partner in diffusing the anger you feel toward each other, in non-destructive ways.

There are two types of anger: **Current Anger** and **Repressed Anger**.

Current Anger is anger arising spontaneously in response to a present situation, where your needs or desires are not being fulfilled. It is a powerful emotional force that demands to be expressed. Current Anger also informs you when someone has physically or emotionally violated your personal boundaries. If it is clearly and effectively expressed,

Current Anger can protect you from harm and sharply define your limits or boundaries to another. Because of the vitality of Current Anger, it's important to learn safe methods of communicating it to others.

Anger will never disappear so long as thoughts of resentment are cherished in the mind.
Anger will disappear just as soon as thoughts of resentment are forgotten.
Buddha, (568-488 BC),
Founder of Buddhism.

Repressed Anger is accumulated anger which has never been released. Layer upon layer of unexpressed Current Anger builds up in a swamp of stagnant emotions. Repressed Anger is the pure poison of resentment. These resentments are extremely toxic to personal relationships because they are the major barriers to intimacy.

We wouldn't hold on to resentments unless there were a payoff for us. Often we are unwilling to let go of resentments because they become reusable weapons that we can drag out to emotionally beat our partner back into submission. These resentments from the past, which we continue to use against our partner, are a way to manipulate our partner by producing a continual state of guilt for previous actions. This method of releasing anger is to allow our repressed resentments to slowly ooze out in measured poisonous doses which can be used against our partner over long periods.

Excessive niceness often hides excessive anger

Another very destructive method of releasing resentments is to allow them to build to the point where we discharge them all at once in a giant explosion. This eruption of force can cause great damage to others. It reminds me of Mount St Helens, which everyone thought was a long dead, "nice" volcano. They built beautiful ski trails on its slopes until one day she unexpectedly blew her top.

It's similar to the human situation, when we read in the newspaper that a quiet, humble milkman took out 25 of his customers with an Uzi. The neighbors invariably say, "We are so shocked because he was such a 'nice' man who never had a harsh word to say about anyone."

If you have the exploding type of anger, an antidote to the Mount St Helens scenario is to pattern yourself on the Hawaiian volcanoes. Everyone can go to the edge of the erupting volcano and not get hurt because it's constantly releasing its "repressed" lava.

Some of us repress anger because we fear our partner's reaction if we let it out. So it stays held within, eventually leaking out in passive-aggressive ways, which can do just as much harm as a direct approach.

> Anger: an acid that can do more harm to the vessel in which it is stored than to anything on which it is poured.
> Seneca, (4 B.C. – 65 A.D.), Roman statesman, philosopher.

Sarcasm and gossip are two very destructive passive-aggressive methods of releasing repressed anger. Sarcasm is especially deadly because its blade is hidden in a sheath of laughter. When it's directed towards us, we immediately sense an attack. When we glance around the room, it's usually confirmed because we're the only one who is not laughing.

Sarcasm is for cowards because it's a hit-and-run operation where they smack you with their resentment and then run into the bushes to hide behind their pitiful attempt at humor. If you were to confront the sarcastic person by asking them why they said it, you'd probably get a response like, "What's the matter, mate, you can't take a little joke?" A way to diffuse sarcasm is to confront the person directly by asking if they are angry with you and stating that you would appreciate it if they would stop using sarcasm at your expense. They will usually deny it but you have at least put them on notice that you are aware of their resentment.

Gossip is another way of passively releasing anger. We have all done it at one time or another. It's hard to resist because we all want to hear the juicy goods on another. We're attracted to the gossip and yet we lose respect for the person doing the gossiping. It's especially negative because the person we are gossiping about is not present to defend himself. If you have an issue with someone, speak to that person about your complaint directly. Gossip serves no purpose other than to hurt someone by spreading rumors behind their back. Repressed anger toward another individual is the cause. Only complain directly to the person who has the power to take care of your complaint. Otherwise your complaint to others is just gossip.

Talking Stick reduces tension levels

If you want intimacy and fulfillment in your relationship then it's essential that you let go of all stored resentments or repressed anger.

The **Talking Stick** can be of great assistance in creating a safe environment in which you can express those feelings of resentment to your partner. It's a very effective tool for communicating either Current or Repressed Anger to each other in a gentle way which causes no harm. It may take time to release the backlog of anger so don't rush things by trying to dump it all at once.

As long-held resentments are expressed, a new level of vitality and warmth will be felt in your relationship. Positive feelings will arise which will bring you into closer connection with your partner. It's hard to experience passion within your relationship when a backlog of resentment blocks the free flow of feeling between you.

Agreeing to disagree

Most couples are afraid to argue and when they finally do, it's not done well. That's the bottom line. We are generally afraid of the vitality and energy of anger and the potential harm it may cause, so we choose to deny and suppress it. Eventually it will be expressed one way or another.

The energy of anger is potentially liberating if handled with care. There is very little difference between anger, passion, and physical vitality. It's just energy expressed in different ways. If you're blocking anger, you are blocking your feelings of passion. It's impossible to feel alive and passionate in a relationship if you and your partner are withholding anger.

"We never fight"

I often hear people say, "We've never had an argument," as if they should be awarded some special medal for not fighting. More than likely there is a lack of passion and healthy sexual response within the relationship. Blocked anger equals blocked sexual energies.

It's important to strive for harmony within your relationship, but not at a cost of suppressing and denying your mutual anger. It's inevitable that tensions will arise between two individuals sharing an intimate relationship in today's stressful culture.

Bringing those tensions out into the open is infinitely healthier than withholding your grievances for the sake of some so-called ideal of perfect harmony. Assertively communicating your differences to each other by using the safety of the Talking Stick will regenerate an aliveness and passion that was missing from your relationship.

"We always fight"

On the other hand, some couples argue continually with each other. Little disagreements often escalate into major confrontations which are hard to control. Usually it's about controlling each other, with anger as your weapon of choice. No one is listening and everyone is talking at the same time.

A lack of passion is not the problem here. The problem is a lack of control. Being in a state of continual war, a couple will have a tendency to burn each other out until they reach the point of total exhaustion. This results in a negative impact on their sexuality because there isn't any energy left for passion. The constant battles and verbal attacks eventually damage the relationship beyond repair.

The Talking Stick is a perfect tool for cooling down the excess heat of anger. If used correctly, it naturally slows down the communication process and prevents the needless escalation of anger. The Talking Stick will assist you in expressing your anger in measured, digestible amounts which your partner can accept without feeling provoked.

Using the Talking Stick at the beginning of a disagreement diffuses any rising tension between you and your partner before it escalates into a full blown argument. Often, just listening to each other immediately reduces the chances of a major confrontation.

Fighting Fair

In an attempt to make the insanity of war more civilized, most nations of the world decided to sign a document called the Geneva Convention. This document was designed to prevent atrocities such as genocide or other inhumane treatment from occurring during times of war (the ultimate oxymoron, civilized war).

When it comes to our most intimate relationship battles, we don't have any agreement with our partner which would prevent us from causing excessive emotional harm to each other. It's essential to create your own "Geneva Convention" type of agreement for your relationship. If both of you agree to abide by the rules of this agreement, you will discover the ability to disagree and argue fairly while not hurting each other in the process.

Rules of Engagement

- **Stay on the issue** – Do not bring up issues that are unrelated to the topic being discussed. Often a person will avoid talking about an uncomfortable topic by changing the issue. It's very important to resolve the issue being argued before moving on to another one.

- **Speak in "I" messages** – Your arguments will be better received by your partner if you speak about your feelings using the first person. Taking responsibility for your own feelings by saying "I feel..." instead of "You made me..." reduces the possibility of your partner feeling blamed or judged and becoming defensive. Your partner can certainly challenge your judgment if you call him "stupid." However, if you rephrase your words to talk about how you felt because of his action, he can't tell you how you should feel because your feelings are yours.

There are three parts to effective "I" messages:
1. **When** (describes the action that affects you).
2. **I feel** (explains how you feel).
3. **Because** (gives the reason for your feelings).
   > **Incorrect:** "You always throw your dirty clothes on the floor."
   > **Correct (I message):** "**When** you toss your dirty clothes on the floor, **I feel** angry, **because** I'll have to pick them up."
   > **Incorrect:** "You're late again because you only think about yourself first."
   > **Correct (I message):** "**When** you're late, **I feel** angry, **because** it appears you don't value my time."

- **Avoid using absolutes** – Words used to describe your partner's behavior such as "always," "never," "forever," and "constantly," are inflammatory by nature and will tend to provoke anger. How can a person defend themselves against words like never or always? Don't exaggerate in order to add weight to your argument. Words such as "sometimes," "often," or "occasionally" are usually a more accurate description of the frequency of a transgression than using words that reflect eternity.

- **Don't rehash the past** – It's not fair to use resentments from the past as a battering ram to beat your partner into submission. The past is over and gone so let it rest in peace. If you often find yourself bringing up past grievances then it's important for you to do release work around those resentments and let them go once and for all.

- **Use timeouts** – If anger escalates out of control, it's important for one of you to call a timeout. When one partner feels that a timeout is necessary then it's important for you both to agree to let it go until a better time. Walk away from the argument until you have both calmed down. It's useless to attempt to communicate with each other when you're both screaming like a couple of banshees.

- **Never use violence** – Anger is a powerful emotion and if you get to a place where you're pushing each other around physically then it's time to immediately walk away and defuse the situation. There is never a justification for using any physical force on your partner. Both men and women are capable of causing serious bodily harm to each other. If you find that it's hard for you to stop using physical force on your partner then it's imperative that you seek professional support and counseling immediately because you're kidding yourself if you think you can handle it.

- **Avoid verbal abuse** – Calling your partner obscene names or using derogatory statements such as "You're stupid" are aggressive acts of emotional abuse. Even though you can't see the emotional scars, your sharp words have left a deep wound on your partner's soul. Criticize the action or behavior but not the total person. For example, say "When you tell me not to wear my short dress, I feel as if you're trying to control me, because I want to choose what I want to wear," instead of, "You are such a control freak."

- **Stop raising your voice** – It's natural to have a little intensity in your voice when you're having an argument but excessively raising the volume can cause your argument to escalate into a full-fledged battle.

Keep reminding each other to tone your voices down if matters start getting out of hand. Shouting each other down will only make the situation worse than what it was before you started talking and leave both of you with hurt feelings.

- **Remember the love** – No matter how heated the argument, remember that the person you're feeling angry toward is a person you love. In the middle of a fight your partner may appear on the surface to be your mortal enemy and you're questioning your judgment in making such a foolish decision as to be in the relationship in the first place. In actuality, your partner loves you so much that he or she is willing to withstand some of your greatest outbursts and still be standing shoulder to shoulder with you the following day. Below the surface, there are deeper spiritual forces at work to assist both of you in healing much of the pain from the past which caused the anger to begin with.

> Never go to bed angry, stay up and fight.
> Phyllis Diller, (1861-1951),
> American columnist.

With both of you agreeing to the Rules of Engagement, the quality of your relationship will dramatically improve because of the safe expression of anger within your union. Long-held resentments can be released once and for all, clearing the way to newfound passions and a transformed stream of love between you. Signing the following agreement to Fight Fair creates an agreement between you to disagree and argue about various issues while maintaining mutual love and respect for each other. Sign this agreement only if you are sincere in your intention to approach your differences with love and fairness by abiding by the Rules of Engagement.

> There's nothing wrong with anger provided you use it constructively.
>
> Wayne Dyer, (1940 -),
> American psychotherapist, author, lecturer.

Rules of Engagement – Fighting Fair

As Intimate Partners,
we_____

and_____ agree to abide by
these **Rules of Engagement**:

I agree:
- to stay on the issue.
- to speak in "I" messages.
- to avoid using absolutes such as 'always' and 'never'.
- to not bring up the past.
- to use timeouts.
- to never use violence.
- to avoid verbal abuse.
- to remember the love.

_____   _____
         Partner   Partner
              Signatures
_____   _____
         Date   Date

Chapter 7

Withholds

Between whom there is hearty truth, there is love.
Henry David Thoreau, (1817-1862),
American essayist, poet, naturalist

Withholds are the various unexpressed thoughts and feelings that, for whatever reason, you're not willing to communicate to your partner.

Withholds will slowly destroy the fabric and foundation of your relationship as surely as termites can eat away at your house unseen.

Withholds are the single most toxic poison that we experience in a relationship. The communication of your personal truth, no matter how concerned you are about the way that truth will be received by your partner, is the only antidote.

One of the primary reasons we withhold anything in the first place is the fear of reprisal from our partner if we communicate our repressed feelings. We're afraid they may retaliate with anger and rejection if they don't like what we have to say.

It can be a relatively small annoyance like your wife keeps forgetting to stack the dishwasher, or you feel insecure about your husband's new secretary. We ignore these feelings and refuse to speak to each other about our concerns. Layer upon layer of withholds continue to accumulate until the burden becomes unbearable and then we explode in an argument or even leave the relationship.

Perhaps you say, "What's the use of talking, he just ignores me?" Maybe your partner uses anger to stop you, so you say, "If I bring this up with her she's going to flip out so

I'll just sit on it." And sit on it we do, as the withholds slowly accumulate over time until we have a reservoir of stagnant, unexpressed emotions.

If we can't communicate the little things that disturb us in our relationship, how will we ever deal with the very important ones?

For example, if you can't tell your husband that his snoring irritates you, how the hell are you going to tell him that you have the hots for the mailman? If you won't tell your son that you can't play with him because you'd rather be alone for a while, there's no way that you can tell him that his pet turtle didn't actually die by falling off the balcony but that you actually flattened the little fellow with your brand new boots. As you can see, there is an endless range of possible feelings which we can withhold from our loved ones.

All emotions and feelings are energy. If you have any doubt about the energetic charge of emotions, consider the power of love and anger. You may have to search your memory banks, but remember the intense feelings of love that flowed when you gazed into your lover's eyes and kissed deeply for the first time? Felt a little excited? Love acts as a powerful magnet which attracts you to another. On the other hand, anger is a powerful emotion that repels. Just consider how you felt the last time you really lost your temper. Felt a little energized?

Emotion = E ~Motion = Energy in Motion = The Movement of Energetic Feeling

Withholds are like a dam, restricting the free movement of emotions we could be expressing openly to our partner. When that dam swells, the feeling connection between you and your partner begins to deteriorate. It's a slow process and eventually we drift further and further from our friend until the day comes where we feel we're not in love anymore and start looking for a door out.

Clearing withholds is the key

Withholds create a swamp of stagnant, unexpressed feelings that smother the life out of your relationship. The key to draining the swamp is to get those waters of love flowing again by communicating your withholds to your partner on a regular basis. As dam gates need to be periodically opened in order to keep the water in the reservoir from overflowing, you have to release your emotions so that anger and resentments don't spill over and hurt the one you love.

A good method of discharging withholds is to keep a small spiral notepad nearby, so you can jot down issues arising between you and your partner that disturb or upset you. Keep recording items of stress between you and your partner which you would like to express and clear at a more appropriate time.

The reason for taking the time to write things down is that often issues come up at inappropriate times when you are busy with the daily pressures of life. Unless it's a big issue that needs to be dealt with on the spot, most withholds can be recorded and communicated to each other at a more suitable time.

Clearing sessions using the Talking Stick

For the next 3 months, schedule a 15 minute weekly withholds clearing meeting where you each get out your withholds pad and use the Talking Stick to express those thoughts and feelings which were written down. Quite often there may be no withholds recorded or one partner may have a list three pages long! Either way, you get in the habit of sharing a weekly session with your partner. Eventually you become up to date with your withholds and there remains nothing left to be withheld from each other. That's the goal.

As with the Talking Stick, it's very important to schedule your weekly withhold meeting when you have at least 15 minutes of complete privacy with no interruptions, children or cell phones. A withholds session can be called for by either partner if needed at any time.

Most the time we don't even know how much we're withholding. The first step is to be brutally honest with ourselves by looking within and seeing if we have any residual anger, hurts or fears that we are not sharing with our partner.

Because a lot of this emotional clearing is small stuff, it will be relatively easy to mutually express your withholds.

A small percentage of withholds will hold a large emotional charge. It's important that you respect the rules of the Talking Stick and communicate those sticky feelings with as much grace and caring as you can muster.

Remember, no matter how angry you are at your partner or how deeply hurt you may be, it's important to remember that you hold each other in a place of respect and love.

The more you clear withholds, the easier it becomes. Initially, when you begin the clearing process, the reservoir of repressed feelings is full to the brim. The weight of your emotional reservoir lightens up as you begin to release old feelings through the communication process. The gigantic emotions of frustration, sorrow and fear are safely discharged through the clearing process.

If you stick with this process, you'll be surprised and delighted in feeling a personal sense of empowerment from speaking your truth. You will experience renewed interest in your partner because of the cleared emotional field between you.

We humans can withhold in storage an amazing amount of thoughts and feelings which eventually create heaviness in our soul. We become emotionally obese.

The only way to lose that emotional weight is by continually shedding those heavy feelings through clear and honest communication of the issues that you're withholding from your partner.

When that occurs you'll feel the waters of love move between you again in an ever increasing flow, and instead of sitting in a swamp of stagnant emotion caused by your withholds, you will both begin to experience a fast running stream of feelings regenerating your relationship.

Expressing your mutual withholds to each other is vital to the endurance and strength of your relationship. The Talking Stick gives you the safety and framework in which to do it.

Clearing withholds on a regular basis is a cornerstone of this book. If you truly want to experience more well-being in your relationship, along with lots more passion, then continue to persevere in releasing the storage pit of your withholds on a regular basis.

The rewards will be far beyond your expectations.

PART II

Supportive Relationship Concepts

Chapter 8

Emotional Time Bombs

One of the oddest features of western Christianized culture is its ready acceptance of the myth of the stable family and the happy marriage. We have been taught to accept the myth not as a heroic ideal, something good, brave, and nearly impossible to fulfill, but as the very fiber of normal life. Given most families and most marriages, the belief seems admirable but foolhardy.

Jonathan Raban, (1942 -),
British author, critic.

From my experience, the only way to enjoy deep fulfillment in an intimate relationship is to take the time to search within and heal your emotional wounds from the past. Unresolved emotional needs from your childhood will interfere in your ability to fully give and receive love in your relationship.

Sure, you can have a relatively healthy relationship with another person and not ever look within to see if there are any emotional issues which need to be healed. In fact, many couples have been together for a considerable number of years as a happy functioning couple.

Are those relationships as richly fulfilling and joyful as they could be if a little attention were paid to inner emotional homework? I don't think so.

> The easiest way to solve a problem is to
> deny that it exists
> Isaac Asimov (1920-1992)
> Writer, Scientist

I can hear some of you say, "Wait a minute Des! I don't have any issues from my childhood. My family was absolutely normal, my parents were fine in the way they raised me, and I think you're mistaken." Maybe I am. If so, I apologize because you may be that one child in a million who was lucky enough to have had a perfect childhood. To you I say congratulations and I'm glad that you don't have to encounter any trials and tribulations in your relationships. Things must be flowing well in your life and especially in your relationships so I think you made a mistake by picking up this book because everything is normal, and you and your partner never have a glitch, right?

If you're on Earth, you've got issues

Normal behavior does not always equate to healthy behavior, especially since the emotional norm on planet Earth is extremely low. Sometimes it's better to look at the bigger picture to gain a proper perspective on things, so before we look at some of the difficulties that our emotional imbalances create in our intimate relationships, let's consider the world stage.

Until the middle of the 20th century, personal inner growth and looking within ourselves to heal deep-seated emotional wounds was certainly not the custom. Survival was the order of the day and only the rich or the artistic had time for inner reflection. We were emotionally unconscious.

As mankind has been freed from the toils of labor, we have enjoyed more time, at least in our Western culture, to start looking within and reflecting on our inner nature, which includes our emotional needs and responses. The science of psychology has discovered that most of us are underdeveloped in our emotional growth and maturity.

As a species, our intellectual quotient (IQ) has leap-frogged way beyond the accumulated mental accomplishments of the previous centuries. In just one century, our fastest mode of transportation progressed from the train, which could take us from point A to point B at top speeds of about 70 mph, to the jet rocket, which traveled to the moon and back at speeds of 25,000 mph.

In medicine, we progressed from opening bodies without anesthesia to successfully saving lives by transplanting vital organs such as the liver and the heart. This intellectual leap in mental maturity was unprecedented in the history of mankind. We seem to have come of age with our mental expertise and abilities.

Emotionally, humanity is a 14 year old

Our emotional quotient, EQ, appears to be stunted in comparison to its intellectual brother, IQ. Emotionally, we haven't progressed much past puberty as a measure of maturity. Our massive intellectual progress has been both a blessing and a curse.

On a national scale, this emotional immaturity has produced devastating consequences. Nations have relationships with other nations in much the same way that individual human beings relate to other individual human beings. These national relationships can be positive ones, creating trade links, peace treaties, a strong flow of goodwill and a healthy social intercourse between the separate countries. Nations can also have negative relationships with other countries, producing suspicion, poor communication, and conflicting political structures which can eventually lead to war. The same is true for our individual human relationships. They are either positive or negative in nature.

Mankind learned how to split the atom and, because of our low EQ, quickly invented the atomic bomb. In the middle of the huge collective temper tantrum called World War II, we indiscriminately exploded this monstrosity on our fellow women, men and children. This was the inevitable result of giving big boys big toys which can do big harm.

The 20th century was probably the bloodiest and most inhumane in the history of mankind. Humans produced two global world wars and for the first time in history destroyed civilian population centers on a massive scale. The atrocities man committed against man have been unprecedented in the history of the planet. This occurred because of our intellectual maturity and our emotional immaturity.

We have the intellectual capacity to create incredible technologies and yet at this point in time we lack the emotional wisdom which would allow us to safely use them.

As nations are made up of millions of individuals, wars will continue between nations until we each individually learn to establish balance within our emotional inner life. As a species, we are headed in the direction of emotional maturity but it appears that humanity's progression through our "terrible teen" years will create a few gigantic dramas in the world arena before we get there.

On a smaller scale, the emotional global immaturity, with all its destructive tendencies, is mirrored in our individual one-on-one relationships. Intimate relationships, with their extremely high divorce rates, physical and emotional spousal hostility, child abuse, rampant depression, and overall lack of joy, mimic the behavior of nations.

Of course, not all relationships reflect such negativity, just as many nations never go to war. I'm just trying to establish the fact that as a species, human beings have a lot of growing up to do.

From the global stage to the local stage

You are a product of your hereditary potentials, the emotional environment of your childhood, and the inner spiritual blueprint of your destiny. Our society causes great difficulty when it idealizes the "perfect family." A huge gap exists between the ideal vision of the happy family and the pain and dysfunction of the average one. When we start our own family, we are unprepared for the emotional realities that await us.

When it comes to intimate relationships, the emotional

imprint from your family of origin has a massive influence on your ability to enjoy a healthy emotional life. The early childhood environment in which you were raised, and the emotional health of your parents, greatly affects your ability to love yourself and others.

Please understand this is not a judgment of your mother or father's parenting abilities. Your parents did the very best they could to nurture you in childhood. Let's not forget that each previous generation had it much tougher than you did when they were kids. You and your parents have not only inherited your physical attributes from your ancestors, but you've also inherited the emotional patterns and complexes from your family's extensive past.

Everything in this world of duality is a mixture of both plus and minus, good and bad. Because life on Earth has been incredibly difficult until recently, your emotional inheritance largely consists of a chain of pain that has been passed down from parent to child for countless generations. No one talks about it because most of us aren't even aware of this emotional inheritance.

Why do you think you see all those sour-looking faces in the first family photographs in the last part of the 19th century? It sure looked as if no one were having any fun. It's important for you to remember how tough it was for your parents and even tougher for the generations before them, to grow up in a healthy emotional environment. The next time you feel excessively judgmental toward your parents, remember those old depressive-looking photos from the 1800s.

If as a child you were not taught how to love and accept the beauty of your being, then as you become an adult it will be just as difficult to love and accept the beauty of another.

In my own situation, I have three amazing daughters and one totally switched-on stepson I love as if he were my own son. If you were to ask me if I were the perfect father to my children, I'd have to say not by a long shot. If you were to ask my children how I did, they would probably say at times when they needed me, I wasn't there for them. However, I'm sure they don't have any doubt about how much I love them, although I probably should have set up a trust fund for any future counseling which they may need to heal any damage my lack of parenting skills may have done. Yet I love my children deeply and I can see that, as I emotionally matured, my ability to nurture my children improved with time. I think it's safe to say that my kids will also strive to always be there for their children, but sometimes they will probably miss the mark a few times themselves. It's just the nature of our human condition, because our parenting skills reflect our own emotional well-being and our ability to give and receive love.

Emotional time bombs ticking away

As a child, you had a deep need for total love and acceptance from your parents. Your parents attempted to fill those needs to the best of their ability. Quite often, they weren't able to do so and you were left with unfulfilled needs at various times during your childhood. These unfulfilled emotional needs have a tendency to lay dormant for many years until unexpectedly exploding in the middle of your adult relationships.

As you grow into an adult, you unconsciously attempt to satisfy those unfulfilled childhood needs through your intimate relationships. This puts an enormous pressure on your partner in the relationship because your partner is in the same situation as you. Your partner is attempting to have unfulfilled childhood needs satisfied by you. How can you or your partner take care of each other's emotional needs when neither one of you was taught how to take care of your own needs? It's usually at this point that you start blaming your partner for not caring enough about your needs and the cycle of blame and accusation begins.

Until we become aware of the unresolved issues from our childhood and learn how to begin to heal them, we will continually encounter lack of fulfillment and trouble in our relationships.

Searching for fulfillment

Have you ever wondered why it feels so fantastic to fall in love with another human being? When you discover someone who's totally interested in everything you say and do, everyday life takes a back seat to the pursuit of your budding intimate relationship. Levels of trust build to the point where you both feel safe enough to lower the defensive walls around your hearts. It's still scary because you're both totally exposed and yet you push on in your desire to merge with your beloved.

As you gaze into your lover's eyes, waves of joy ripple through you and the most amazing euphoric feelings pump through your body with every beat of your heart. Your brain releases massive amounts of chemical endorphins, which quickly send you to Cloud Nine. Finally, someone totally sees you and their unconditional acceptance of what they see is nothing short of miraculous.

The mutual choice to lower your defenses has allowed each of you to see a part of you that rarely sees the light of day, the most vulnerable and beautiful part of your being, the Inner Child. It's called the Inner Child because the word Child represents a time in your life when you were innocent, totally open, joyful, playful, trusting and incredibly sensitive. This Inner Child embodies all of your feelings. It is the most magical part of your humanity because it is the spark of divinity which gives you your unique individuality. When you and your partner allow each other to see the exquisite beauty of your Inner Children, you both tap into one of the most fundamentally powerful drives that a human can experience, the desire to be seen and loved unconditionally. The only other time that you have ever experienced feelings similar to romantically falling in love is when you first came to this planet as a newborn baby. As an infant, you experienced total acceptance for the first time with your mother and father and for a while you felt totally loved, accepted and nurtured. Everyone loved you, the cute new baby in the family, and you felt totally safe and fulfilled.

Everything was going fine and you were blossoming in a

steady fountain of love flowing from the care of your parents. As you started to express your own individuality and began to challenge parental authority, the inevitable started to occur. Because of the stresses of life and the disharmony present in your parent's emotional nature, they may have responded to your challenges by expressing the powerful emotions of anger, fear and sorrow in destructive ways which had a potent negative impact on you as a young child.

Sometimes you needed more nurturing and unconditional love than your parents were able to give. Other dynamics of the family such as the natural competitive interaction with brothers and sisters also caused you to pull back energetically to protect your sensitive heart by feeling less. In other words, you started to reduce your level of openness by numbing your emotions to lessen the level of your sensitivity.

Your parents were doing the very best they could but at times it wasn't enough and many of your emotional needs were probably unfulfilled in one way or another. It's these unfulfilled emotional needs from childhood that cause trouble in your adult intimate relationships because you unconsciously attempt to have those needs fulfilled by your partner.

> In real love you want the other person's good. In romantic love, you want the other person.
> Margaret Anderson, (1886 – 1973),
> Editor, author.

You see, when you're in that heady stage of initial love, your defenses are completely down and everything is wonderful. On a deeper level, your soul has recreated a similar situation to your childhood where you're depending on another human being to fulfil your emotional needs.

On the surface you and your partner are deeply connecting with each other and it feels great, but below the surface there is an unconscious agreement between you that says, "I'll take care of your inner emotional needs if you take care of mine." You're able to do this for a while but eventually you both become exhausted from constantly attempting to fill each other's emotional needs. The truth is; how are you going to take care of someone else's Inner Child when you don't know how to take care of your own?

This is when you both start to emotionally withdraw from each other as your Inner Child retreats to safer ground and the feelings that were special, magical, and alive vanish into thin air. The intense feelings of connection that you experienced at the start of your relationship are nowhere to be found. Now is about the time that you resign yourself to a relationship that's far less than you had expected, or you start looking for a way out.

Healing the past

The only way to prevent your Inner Child from checking out of your relationship is to start looking within and learn how to take care of your own emotional needs. In other words, you must learn how to re-parent your Inner Child.

Basically, what this means is a shift from looking for others to take care of your primary emotional needs, to learning how to provide for your own inner needs.

Now I don't want to create any illusions that this will be an easy process. Learning how to take care of your Inner Child is a lifelong lesson and at times it can be especially difficult. There are a few reasons why it will take a little time for you to get to a place of being able to take care of yourself more successfully.

Our whole culture is set up with a focus on being outer directed. What I mean is that since you were a Child, you were taught to emotionally and physically depend on others for your survival. Even as you grew older and survival was not an issue, you still were seeking from your family and friends the approval and love you desired so deeply.

We hear the phrase unconditional love tossed around a lot these days. We did get a little bit of that when we were young but, by and large, the majority of the love that we received from others was very conditional. All too often, we find that if we did exactly what Mommy and Daddy wanted, everything was fine and the love flowed. But the moment we chose to rock the boat and challenge our parents' directives, that strong flow of love would dry up to a trickle as our parents would shut off their love by emotionally withdrawing their connection. This terrified us and we would have done anything to re-establish their love for us. (That's why it's vital in raising your children to never use love as a bargaining chip in getting them to do what you want. Show disapproval, anger or disappointment at their actions but always distinguish between the individuality of the child and the child's behavior. Let them know that you love them in spite of their disobedience.)

Being taught to depend on others for a source of nurturing and not being given the skills to nurture yourself has left you at an emotional disadvantage because it leaves you much too dependent on the willingness of others to provide for your emotional health.

Dependency is the door to manipulation

When you desperately want love from another and the other person knows it, it puts you at a great disadvantage because this person could use guilt and manipulation to get you to do whatever it is they want. In other words, their love goes up for auction. Because you are dependent on this person's love, you can't help but give in to their manipulation in order to get the love you need.

The quickest antidote to emotional manipulation is learning how to provide for your emotional needs yourself. In learning how to take care of your own Inner Child, you may be disappointed if love is withdrawn but you won't be desperate. By filling your own emotional cup, you won't be led around by the nose because of someone else's manipulative strategies.

It's the only path to true emotional freedom within a relationship, because by filling your own emotional well, you are no longer at the mercy of other human beings who may or may not give you what you need.

Tearing down walls – drawing boundaries

Boundaries is a term used to describe physical, mental, or emotional limits that are drawn with another person. Boundaries are important because they define the limits of what you feel is important to you within your relationship.

For example, setting a physical boundary may be telling your partner that under no circumstances would you allow him or her to physically assault you. An example of an emotional boundary could be the request that your partner reveal to you any serious physical attraction experienced for another person when it occurs. In order to define our limits as a human being to another soul it's important for us to have a healthy sense of self. It's very difficult to set boundaries when we really don't understand what our emotional and physical needs are. We learn how to define our boundaries as we discover the needs and wants of our Inner Child. Until the time when we can consciously protect ourselves by setting boundaries, the usual way we protect ourselves is by building very strong walls.

Walls are solid structures and boundaries are porous ones. For example a typical wall may look something like this: A man has repeatedly requested his wife to call home if she is going to be late and again she shows up at home two hours late without giving him a call. The wife arrives home and can immediately sense that her husband is angry and she says, "What's wrong dear? Are you angry with me?" He gives her a dirty look and says, "I don't want to talk about it. I'm going to bed." Again she asks, "Are you upset that I didn't call you?" Once again he says, "I told you I'm going to bed and I have nothing to say." The husband retreats to the bedroom feeling angry and hurt that his wife again neglected to call him.

In the same situation, a boundary could be expressed this way. The wife arrives home and can immediately sense that her husband is angry and she says, "What's wrong dear? I feel that you're angry with me." He responds, "Sharon, your feelings are right because I am angry. When you didn't call me to let me know that you were going to be late, I felt very upset because you promised me that you would call. I am strongly asking that you honor your commitment to call me if you're going to be late because it's very important to me. Will you honor this?" The wife, seeing how important it is to her husband for her to call says "I'm sorry and I'll honor your request to call you when I'm going to be late." The husband is overjoyed at his wife's understanding and sweeps her into his arms, passionately kissing her as he picks her up and hungrily carries her to the bedroom for a night of unforgettable lovemaking. As he gently lays her on the bed, she looks up into his eyes and says, "I am so glad that we read that wonderful book, *21st Century Relationship Guide*, because none of this would be happening if we hadn't." (Oops...looks like I got carried away. Let's see, where was I?) In the first example of a wall, the man shuts down, stores his hurt and anger, and doesn't inform his wife of his boundary in the situation of her being late. In the second example, the husband expresses his feelings and strongly draws a line in the sand about his wife's behavior. The wife now knows her husband's spoken limit or boundary and has chosen to respect that boundary by calling home next time.

Walls are created so that we may protect our Inner Child from getting hurt and yet because of their solidity, they have a tendency to block most of our feelings and emotional numbness is the result.

Boundaries are a different kind of protection because they are always present when you need them but they allow the free flow of feelings to take place unencumbered.

Another way that we create walls is by numbing out with drugs and alcohol in order to deaden the pain of our stored sorrow and anger. Nicotine, alcohol, marijuana and stronger drugs give us temporary relief from our inner pain because we become anaesthetized. This self medication comes at an enormous cost to our health, our happiness and our intimate relationships. We become walking emotional zombies, unaware of our total lack of feeling.

It doesn't matter what causes the walls to go up. What

matters is that we learn how to knock them down by getting to the roots of our pain and releasing it once and for all. Emotional inner work is the only path to emotional health.

I know all about walls as I had constructed rock solid ones around my heart for many years. Walls are very effective at keeping the baddies out. The only problem is, walls aren't very discriminating and they wind up keeping the goodies out too. In fact, no one could get close to me because they couldn't get past my walls. I remember various people pounding on them and yelling, "Hello! Is there anybody in there?" I felt safe but I also felt very lonely. It wasn't until I started looking within and healing emotional patterns from the past that I felt safe enough to start lowering my walls and replacing them with strong healthy boundaries.

As we become emotionally healthy, boundaries are a much more effective protection because we put them up only when necessary, and when the danger is past we can let down our guard and engage the world.

Boundaries are vital in your intimate relationships because they tell you and your partner just how far each of you can go without hurting each other. Until you become more comfortable with your emotional life, it is very difficult to set strong boundaries with your partner. As long as you're depending on another person for your source of love, you will always be super cautious about saying too much of your truth or expressing too much of your anger to your partner. Your Inner Child is terrified of being abandoned by the one you love. You're afraid that if your partner doesn't like what you said, they may run away. Instead of being authentic with your partner and feeling safe enough to speak your absolute truth, you attempt to finesse the relationship by only revealing what you think your partner can handle. This of course will lead to a massive amount of emotional withholds which will drain the very life out of your union. Use the **Talking Stick** as a supportive tool for setting boundaries because it creates a space of safety which allows you to assert those boundaries to your partner with clarity. It's best to do so when you are both relaxed and in a harmonious state of mind.

As you learn to set boundaries in your relationship, don't expect your boundaries to be automatically accepted and respected by your partner. If your partner is not used to you defining your limits, they may blow you off initially by not honoring those limits just out of habit. They may even rebel against your boundary and express anger. Just gently inform your partner that you're working on emotional growth and then repeat your boundary again, asking for your request to be respected. Eventually, if they love you, they will come on board by learning to honor your boundaries.

Distinguish between friend and foe

Quite often when learning to set boundaries we can be scared that if we start saying no to the people in our life, they may get upset with us, withdraw their love and possibly even leave. In actuality, many of your friends and loved ones may not like your newfound strength, but eventually they'll come around because they love you.

Only a small percentage of people in your life will rebel against you asserting your limits with them and refuse to honor your boundaries. Emotional health demands that you eventually let those few so-called friends go because they are toxic and they are certainly not being friends.

If you want to find out who are your true friends in life, start setting boundaries. Your friends will honor your boundaries while the people you thought were your friends won't.

For me, when I set a boundary with an individual, I expect it to be honored. If it isn't, I'll set a stronger boundary with them again. If my boundary is disregarded once more, I'll firmly let them know that I don't feel safe because my limits are being ignored, and if it continues I'll eventually withdraw my energy from the relationship.

For instance, let's say you're irritated because a friend of yours calls you on the phone at 7:30 on Saturday mornings. You have requested over and over not to do so and yet they continue to disregard your request and wake you up. Another example would be your repeated request to your best friend to stop flirting with your husband and she responds by saying you're just being jealous and to get over it.

When you set a boundary with someone and it is dishonored it again and again, what they are communicating to you is that they couldn't care less about your needs. The only thing important to them is what they want. When someone disregards boundaries, your Inner Child will not feel safe so it's important to see the truth of your relationships and let go of the people who are insensitive to your needs.

Interdependency opens a door to freedom

Co-dependency in a relationship is when each person becomes emotionally entwined with the other. This occurs because of the lack of definitive emotional boundaries within the relationship. It's hard to determine your own emotional needs because you can't distinguish between your and your partner's needs. If your emotional limits are not clearly defined with your partner, it will be difficult to assert and fulfill your own individual needs within the relationship.

> Interdependency follows independence.
> Stephen R. Covey,
> Author of The 7 Habits of Highly Effective People.

Interdependency in a relationship is when each person chooses to emotionally merge with the other for the sake of creating a true partnership without letting go of individual emotional independence. This interdependence can only occur if each partner is capable of setting strong limits or boundaries with the other. Interdependency is a reflection of two healthy people consciously choosing to form a romantic joint venture where each can contribute love and energy to the relationship without losing a sense of individuality. The relationship then becomes a true partnership of strong individuals choosing to merge in love for the sake of creating a greater whole. Strength aligned with strength instead of weakness leaning on weakness.

Filling your well

If you want to learn how to create interdependency in your relationship and discover the inner strength to do so, then learning how to take care of your own inner needs is the only way to do it.

This process of learning how to discover your core emotional needs and finding a way to fulfill those needs takes time. Since you have spent years neglecting your inner emotional needs, it will also take a few years to learn how to take care of yourself, so be patient.

Many wonderful books are on the market which can assist you in discovering ways of nurturing yourself.

John Bradshaw's influential book, *Homecoming: Reclaiming and Championing Your Inner Child*, along with Lucia Capacchione's very practical workbook, *Recovery of Your Inner Child*, are two that have assisted me greatly in my own personal healing.

Another favorite of mine is a book which will assist you in rediscovering and expressing your playful and creative Inner Child, *The Artist's Way*, by Julia Cameron.

For some of you, a book will not be adequate because there may be deeper wounds from your past that need to be addressed. You may require the additional support of a professional counselor such as a psychologist who can assist you in uncovering and releasing any previous sorrows. A competent professional healer can show you healthy ways of nurturing and protecting your Inner Child.

In selecting a counselor, it's important to choose someone who is compassionate, empathetic and skilled in teaching you how to reclaim your Inner Child. Enlist your own Inner Child in choosing a counselor by trusting your inner feelings as to whether you feel comfortable with a particular person. If you listen to your feelings, you'll know whether or not you feel safe with the person you have chosen.

Do-it-yourself Inner Child list

Taking care of yourself emotionally doesn't have to be a complex operation. Actually, it can be a very elegant and simple process. Taking care of your Inner Child's needs breaks down into four areas.

If you can learn how to give to yourself many of the items on the following list, I assure you that your life and your relationships will dramatically change for the good.

Your Inner Child requires you:

Physical Safety
-to provide ample food, shelter and physical safety
-to provide lots of play, adventure and physical exercise
-to experience physical affection and touch
-to express and enjoy radiant health
-to explore the physical universe
-to spend time with people you love
-to deeply connect with nature

Emotional Safety
-to be totally accepted and loved
-to be allowed to express and experience all feelings, including anger, sorrow, fear, and joy
-to experience and share laughter
-to be allowed to fully love others
-to be protected from hurtful emotions
-to express enthusiasm
-to experience ecstasy

Mental Safety
-to be protected from harsh criticism
-to be allowed to learn
-to be encouraged often
-to enjoy mental rapport with others
-to dream the big dream and manifest its reality
-to fully express creativity
-to be heard

Spiritual Safety
-to be guided by intuition
-to be totally inspired
-to share inspiration with others
-to feel totally supported by Spirit

-to experience and share the power of spiritual healing
-to merge with Universal Life Energy, God, our Source, our Creator, our life
-to trust that all is well and life is without end

> Take care of the Child in you, and your Child will take care of your dreams.
> Des Coroy.

This is just a partial list of the possible needs of your Inner Child. Please feel free to expand on these possibilities.

If you want to experience the deepest possible connection with another human being, then it's essential for you to explore your inner emotional realms and discover the needs, hopes, and fundamental nature of your Inner Child.

As you learn how to fulfill your inner needs, your capacity to enjoy a strong, rewarding relationship with your intimate partner will be dynamically enhanced by your efforts because you can't demand from your partner what you're not willing to give to yourself.

Chapter 9

My Partner, My Mirror

Behind every silver lining is a grey cloud.
                                        Des Coroy.

As a human being, you possess a mixture of conscious and unconscious personality parts. Many of the unconscious parts of your nature were previously rejected or disowned by you because they caused behaviors which were deemed unacceptable by your family and society. It's the unconscious parts of your being that tend to disrupt the harmony in your relationships. If you want to experience intimacy and harmony in your relationships then it's vital for you to discover, accept, and integrate the disowned parts of you which remain hidden from your awareness. Until you recognize and assimilate the various disowned parts of your being, you will continue to sabotage your relationships and the possibility of profound intimacy will elude you.

There are many different paths which can assist you in discovering the denied parts of your consciousness. Utilizing the skills of a qualified counselor who can guide you on your inner quest of self knowledge is one such path. Another path may be doing your own personal inner growth work such as dream interpretation or journal writing to aid you in understanding the many aspects of the inner you.

One of the most elegant and effective paths for learning about the hidden parts of your nature is to use the powerful technique of seeing your relationships as mirrors.

An idea whose time has come

In 1988 I was in New Orleans supporting my sister Judy, who organized and promoted a dynamic personal growth seminar. The workshop was led by the visionary writer, Shakti Gawain, author of the books *Living in the Light* and *The Path of Transformation*. In attending the event, I noticed Shakti possessed a deep understanding of the undercurrents in relationships. As she was sharing many of her very clear insights, she arrived at the point in her lecture where she explained how our relationships can act as mirrors and it's these mirrors which can assist us in seeing any unconscious parts of our being.

It was one of those "Aha!" experiences where fireworks went off in my head. As she explained further, the elegance and simplicity of the concept excited me. I intuitively knew that using relationships as mirrors was a concept whose time had come on planet Earth and I wanted to be part of sharing it with others. This is one of the most important parts of this book so stay with me and pay close attention to the following words, because I assure you if you learn how to utilize the gifts which your relationships are reflecting to you, you will sidestep future pain and open the door to more harmony, passion, and joy in your life to come.

Your inner family of voices

On the surface, human beings appear to each possess one dominant personality which serves as our primary way of representing ourselves to the world. We tend to be consistent with the way in which we express this personality to others. This primary self, the personality that you identify with the most, is just the tip of the iceberg of who you really are.

My primary self was a "pleaser" who had an ability to sense the needs of my family. This part of me would get love from them by always being "nice." As I grew older, this pleaser part of me became stronger and I became a "nice" guy, which meant that any other parts of me which weren't pleasing to others had to be suppressed, like the angry part of me.

Below the surface you have numerous sub-personalities, both conscious and unconscious, which form the much larger part of your total self. Each one of these sub-personalities or inner voices is representing various, often conflicting, parts of you. For instance, you may have a part of you that is extremely organized and you may have another part of you which prefers chaos to structure. You may have a part of you that is very money conscious and materialistic and a totally different inner voice which identifies with spirituality and going with the flow. You are fully aware of many of these sub-personalities that exist inside, yet you may choose not to reveal them to others. For example, people see you as a confident personality in your business, however you secretly have another part of you which is terrified of failure. Another instance could be that others perceive you as a charming, charismatic lover and yet you have a different part of you which has a great fear of rejection.

In this world of gravity and substance, everything which exists does so in a space of duality. Hot and cold, war and peace, anger and love, tense and relaxed, black and white, are just a few examples of different poles of the same thing. Within our human nature we also have opposite energies existing within our being. Learning to first accept and then balance the many opposites within is the challenge of a lifetime, and perhaps many lifetimes to come.

It's all in the family

This division of your personality into its many polarized sub-personalities began in the family in which you were born and raised. You quickly learned from your parents that some behaviors were acceptable and others were not to be tolerated. You also discovered that some behaviors were rewarded and some were punished.

You began to suppress the parts of you which were causing your parents distress. It didn't take you long to come to an understanding that if you continued to spit your applesauce into mommy's eye, she probably withdrew her love and directed a little anger back your way.

As a youngster you had a greater need for love than you did for milk. You were terrified of losing the energetic connection of love with your parents, so you quickly changed your behavior to win back mommy's love. You began to suppress and deny the parts of you which didn't meet your parents' approval because of the fear of losing their love.

Me and my shadow

In addition to your parental education, schools and religious influences continued to teach you which behaviors were acceptable and which were to be eliminated from your character.

Here's a partial list of some of the negative traits which our society taught us to get rid of or suppress:

Anger is usually one of the first traits deemed unacceptable. You quickly learn that there are big consequences if you continue to beat your little brother's head with a pineapple or if you throw a tantrum at the checkout counter in the local supermarket. The message came through loud and clear that the only ones who had a right to get angry were your parents.

Enthusiasm in a child is a cute quality, but as the child grows enthusiasm becomes annoying to many adults because they dislike and repress the enthusiastic part of themselves. They suppress it in their kids by giving a message such as, "Children should be seen and not heard." Compare the tremendous excitement and energy expressed by a five-year-old to the robotic, self-conscious and measured responses of a young adult.

When children are expressing tremendous vitality and are at their most inquisitive, they are forced to sit in a classroom, relatively motionless, for six hours a day in silence. Many children are falsely diagnosed with Attention Deficit Disorders (ADD) and given powerful drugs when all they're experiencing is a natural and enthusiastic response to being alive. (Note: In my opinion, a rare child may require drugs for behavior control but the percentage is far less than those being prescribed today. I never understood the concept of giving speed to a child who's hyperactive. Diet, food additives, excessive sugar and food allergies are areas to check first before giving a growing child mood-altering drugs. The side effects are usually far worse than the offending behavior. Always question authority.)

Deceit by any means is frowned upon. Theft of property or lying to others is a big no-no and you learn over time to deny, suppress or hide the parts of you which are capable of deception. Manipulation is another form of deceit which you were taught to suppress.

Sexuality in our western-based culture is definitely discouraged in youth. As a child, most of us were trained to associate sexual pleasure with shame.

Greed is counteracted with statements like, "Don't be selfish. Share your toys with your sister," or "You were so greedy when you ate all of the pie and didn't leave any slices for anyone else."

Laziness is particularly frowned upon because idleness does not fit in with our workaholic and materialistic lifestyle.

Meanness is not tolerated because it's the opposite of niceness. One of the first things we learn is that being nice is very important on this planet. Dominating others or using bullying tactics comes under the category of meanness.

This is just a partial list of some of the parts of you that you were taught to eliminate. By the time you became an adult, you disowned or suppressed many parts of you that were judged unacceptable by your parents or society, in order to win the love and approval of others. You became good citizens, purified of the negative parts of your being. This collection of repressed and denied voices is part of your **Shadow Self**.

Everyone is like a moon, and has a dark side which he never shows to anybody.
Mark Twain, (1835 – 1910),
American humorist, writer.

The shadow is a psychological term for all of the aspects of your being that you are unconscious or unaware of. The shadow not only holds the negative parts of you but it also contains positive qualities as well. It's usually the so-called negative parts of the shadow that cause us the most trouble, so for the sake of this chapter we will focus on them. If you want to discover both the positive and negative qualities of your personal shadow then I highly recommend exploring the depths within because that's where you will find your hidden vein of creative gold.

There are some excellent books on the market which can assist you in your quest. Any book by Carl G Jung, the Swiss psychologist who coined the concept of the "shadow", would be an excellent choice. *The Dark Side of the Light Chasers* by Debbie Ford is another excellent book which can assist you in understanding how to reclaim your hidden shadow.

What does this have to do with my relationships?

The shadow has a lot to do with your relationships because those parts of you which you have denied, the not nice parts of your nature that you think you have eliminated, are still within you. They haven't gone away. Nor have you gotten rid of them by killing them off. They're just sitting inside you waiting patiently for your attention and acceptance. No matter how hard you may try get rid of your shadow, it will always be inseparably attached to you. Wherever you go, there it is right behind you, so you might as well make friends with it because it can be a ruthless enemy. Until you come to terms with its existence and come to some kind of peace treaty with your shadow, it will continue to undermine and sabotage the relationships of your life.

In my own life I find that it's easy for me to identify with the parts of me which are generous, truthful, loving and patient but it's much more difficult for me to accept the parts of me which are stingy, deceptive, controlling and manipulative, but believe me they're there. I know these parts of me exist because I have expressed them in the past and have the potential to express them in future.

You may ask why I would want to share the negative aspects of myself with the world? Because it may give you the courage to look within your own self to discover your shadow if I can admit to my own. Our shadows are very similar to each other's anyway. We all tend to put on our very best clothes in public but behind closed doors our shadow reigns and we often wear rags.

This thing of darkness I acknowledge mine.
William Shakespeare, (1564 - 1616),
British poet, playwright, actor.

Your shadow self represents the bottom seven eighths of your personality iceberg, hidden below the surface of your awareness.

Your shadow wants to be included in your consciousness and will do anything to get your attention and acceptance. If you refuse to explore the sub-surface waters of your unconscious and bring light to those denied parts of your being, your inner iceberg will surface in your life at the most unexpected time, causing great damage to the ship of your life.

All of the voices within you, the positive and the so-called negative parts of you, want to be accepted, loved, and included in your total consciousness. We all have sub-personalities that we despise or refuse to accept as ours. These rejected sub-personalities repeatedly come back to haunt us until we finally acknowledge their presence in our lives. I have found the most elegant and powerful way of learning about our inner voices or sub-personalities is the process of Voice Dialogue, developed by Hal and Sidra Stone, PhDs. Their book, *Embracing Each Other*, explains in depth how the various selves of each partner interact in relationships.

One of the primary ways these denied sub-personalities attempt to get our attention is through the arena of relationships.

If you continue to deny and disown these rejected parts of your being, one of the many powerful ways in which the disowned voices can capture your attention is to energetically attract people into your life who have the same qualities as the rejected part of you. You will be both attracted to the reflected qualities of others, and repelled by them at the same time.

Like attracts like

Here is an example to illustrate what I mean. As I mentioned before, for many years of my early life I didn't think that I was angry in any way. I repressed and denied my anger, probably because of my early experience with my father who had a habit of losing his temper. I most likely made an unconscious decision that I would never be angry like him. I saw the destructive aspects of anger and I certainly didn't like it. I denied my anger to the point where I truthfully didn't think it was there. The angry part of me would occasionally show its face by my periodic explosions of temper in some situation. In those moments of rage, it was hard for me to deny that I had anger but I would quickly cut off from those uncomfortable feelings and suppress my anger again.

As I started exploring spirituality, the repression and denial of my anger became more severe because it's certainly not cool for a spiritual person to have anger. I thought that I transcended my anger by meditating it away. It was as if the angry part of me were saying, "I'm here." And I would respond, "No you're not." Finally, the angry voice would say, "Okay, then deal with this!" All of a sudden, I started seeing these angry people showing up in my life everywhere. My wife was angry with me for no apparent reason. My boss was constantly irritated with me at a time when I thought I was doing a good job at work. I couldn't understand why I had these angry, disruptive people around me. For the life of me, I couldn't discover what I was doing to cause them anger.

Because everything vibrates at a certain frequency, the

repressed, angry part of me was magnetically attracting angry individuals whose anger vibrated at the same rate as mine. Physicists call it resonance. When striking a tuning fork, everything nearby tuned to the same frequency will also start to vibrate. It's as if I were a broadcasting from my own station, Radio 2KO Angry FM, and tuning in to every angry person within a radius of 50 miles. My repressed anger was using the medium of relationships to reflect anger back to me as a way of making me aware of my anger within. Because my denial of anger was so strong, at first I didn't understand the reflection. For some time to come I had to put up with the angry people in my life. I remember thinking, "Why is this continuing to happen to me? I'm a nice person and I haven't done anyone harm. I do my morning meditation religiously, balancing on my head with my eyes orbiting my third eye, breathing through my ears while chanting the mantra, 'O-Wa-Ta-Goo-Siam' and people are still angry with me!"

(To discover the hidden meaning of this mantra, repeat it rapidly. Tell no one.)

Eventually I came out of my, "Why me?" victim attitude by finally realizing that maybe the anger out there which was coming at me was only a reflection of what was within my own being. When I took personal responsibility, I could clearly see that I had been storing a lot of anger for a long time. As I started accepting my anger and learned skills to safely express it, I noticed that I was no longer attracting angry people into my life. It was as if the angry part of me said, "Now that I have your attention and you are recognizing my existence, I no longer have to attract these angry people to you." The angry part of me felt accepted at last and no longer had to draw angry mirrors into my life.

Love brings up everything unlike itself to be healed

You have judged some of your sub-personalities as being much too negative or unacceptable to be expressed in society. You then suppressed them to the point where you were no longer aware of their existence. It's these denied or disowned parts of you which create havoc in your close relationships because they want to be accepted into your awareness alongside the so-called good parts of you.

Your soul is continually urging you to become more conscious or aware of all of the different aspects of your being. You grow by discovering, accepting and integrating the various sub-personalities which live within you. Your higher self uses your relationships to make you conscious of the disowned voices within. Most of your relationships serve as mirrors to reflect back to you different aspects of your inner being of which you are not aware.

Physicists tell us that all matter appears to our eyes as solid, but in actuality everything is vibration. Even this book which you're holding in your hand, on the atomic level is pure energy. If everything is vibration, then your emotions and the different parts of your personality are just energy patterns. Because of the power of magnetic attraction, your soul is able to attract people and situations into your life that assist you in evolving toward wholeness in your personality. Whether or not these experiences are pleasurable depends on your acceptance or resistance to your personal growth process.

If you continue to deny your shadow, you often wind up marrying it

Unless you have consciously acknowledged and shared your shadows with each other at the beginning of the relationship, the shadow is guaranteed to surprise both of you later on. It happens to all of us. Your partner will inevitably express the things you dislike and repress most about yourself.

It's a good idea at the start of any intimate relationship to reveal, in measured doses, aspects of your shadow to your potential partner, because your partner will soon discover every hidden part of your shadow anyway. Therefore, you might as well put your cards on the table. If your partner can't handle the totality of who you are, both your light and your dark, at the beginning of the relationship, they won't be able to handle it later. Even worse, if you over identify with the positive aspects of your being to the exclusion of the negative parts of yourself, your partner will mirror the qualities of your shadow back to you on a regular basis.

Having a sexual experience with the negative aspects of your shadow is not the most exciting thing to do in life, or the safest.

Romeo and Juliet had an awful relationship

When we fall in love with another person, for a period from the courtship through the first few years of the relationship you and your beloved both present the brightest parts of your personality to each other. You both shine up your finest attributes and offer them up on the altar of your mutual love.

As you are both still in the courtship or "sales" period of the relationship, the parts of your personality that you reveal to each other are qualities like kindness, generosity, sensitivity, charm, verbal expression, love, fun, spontaneity, romance, fair-mindedness, sexuality, positivity, truthfulness, and humor.

Later, after you have both "closed the deal" by shacking up together or getting married, other parts of your hidden nature begin to surface.

For some couples it may happen slowly over time and for others it comes out all at once. It takes a lot of energy to keep the darker aspects of your shadow under lock and key. As you become more comfortable in the relationship and secure with each other, you begin to relax your guard.

It's usually at this point in the relationship that the prisoners of your unconscious, the shadow parts of you, escape into the light of day. The Darth Vader in you starts to come out with a vengeance. You each discover aspects in the other that you didn't know were there. Attributes begin to surface like meanness, selfishness, deception, boredom, flirting, unfairness, anger, laziness, drunkenness, etc., etc.

Because these black specks of your shadow are contrasted against the lily-white parts of you presented earlier in the relationship, they look especially dark. Usually, this is when you both feel cheated in the relationship because you didn't buy this product at the altar. It feels like the old bait and switch routine, where the best-quality product in the store is advertised and after you purchase it, you notice that an inferior product was switched in its place.

Mirror, mirror on the wall, who has the most denial of all?

If you are determined to suppress your shadow parts and remain in denial of their existence, the mirroring process will come into play and your partner will start to reflect back to you those very aspects of your shadow which you deny. You start seeing your partner as the enemy because if you hate those parts in yourself, you certainly will hate it when it shows up in your partner's behavior and that's when you start the blame game. You can be assured that if you frequently have a strong emotional reaction to personality traits in your partner, there will be a similar but denied part of you lying hidden in your heart.

Let's assume you have a part of your shadow, the controlling part of you, which you have suppressed and denied for many years. As far as you are concerned you don't have a controlling bone in your body. Remembering that all parts of you want to be accepted and are continually trying to get your attention, the repressed controlling part of you attracts a partner into your life who appears to be a very controlling person. Increasingly, you see your partner as being more and more dominant and wanting to control everything. In fact, you get to a point where you can't understand how you have pulled someone into your life that is the exact opposite of you.

This is how the mirroring process works; because of the denial of your own controlling self, you energetically attract a partner into your life that reflects this quality. I can hear you saying, "But Des, you don't understand. It's not my problem because I don't control people, he controls me." We are so used to looking outside of ourselves and blaming others, it is initially difficult for us to begin looking within to determine our responsibility.

> When you judge another, you do not define them, you define yourself.
> Wayne Dyer, (1940 -),
> American psychotherapist, author, lecturer.

In the previous example, the person who feels controlled is not consciously aware of the part of them which may be controlling. Perhaps they have disowned their controlling self many years ago and haven't expressed it in a long time and they don't remember or don't want to remember. Maybe they control their partner through covert or manipulative ways and only view control as direct and assertive domination. There is a part of us all that knows how to get what we want and how to control a person by slinking around in the bushes, so to speak.

If the person who feels controlled took the time to search within, they would discover a controlling part which they may have judged as negative, but it is still there. If they can learn to accept that aspect of their being which they hate so much in their partner, a healing would take place and their partner would no longer affect them in the same way.

When you point the finger of blame you have three fingers pointing back at you

I'll share another example from my life which may clarify the mirroring process. Earlier in the book, I told the story of my resistance to accepting the angry part of me and the problems it created in my life. Once I became aware that my anger was a disowned part of me which I didn't like, I started a long process of learning how to accept and include the angry part of me in my awareness.

Through physical exercise, paying close attention to when anger was building in me and then learning how to release that anger safely, I started to become skilled in how to shift my stored anger into assertive action. Anger was no longer my enemy and it became an ally. I no longer experienced angry people showing up in my life so I felt as if anger were an issue completed once and for all. Then I entered a new relationship with someone I loved. For the sake of this book, we'll call her Sara.

After being together for a while, I thought that Sara was expressing unwarranted anger in our disagreements. As time passed it became a big issue for me and I believed she wasn't playing fair. Of course, I perceived myself to be calm, measured and rational in the way that I expressed my anger with her. Even though Sara was sensing my bottled-up anger, I didn't feel it. I hadn't experienced this much anger in years but because of my previous breakthroughs on anger, I persisted in thinking that she was the culprit. In retrospect, it was my perception of her anger as being excessive, rather than what actually occurred between us, because the issue was primarily mine.

Eventually, the truth of my anger came out of me in a series of gigantic verbal and emotional eruptions which shattered my denial. There is no getting around the physical reality of a temper tantrum. Initially, it's always a bit of a shock to discover parts of you inside that you didn't know were there. No longer would Sara wear the crown of the anger queen that I placed on her when the anger king in me just knocked her off the throne. At least I had the sense not to accuse Sara of making me angry.

What I discovered was a need to take responsibility for the anger in me that I didn't know was present within my relationship with Sara. The angry part of me, which I denied, was trying to get my attention through Sara's anger. In other words, she was expressing not only her own anger but she was also carrying my repressed anger. It wasn't fair to her, especially when I was making her the baddy when she really wasn't.

As I began to assume responsibility for my own anger, I noticed that Sara was less upset about particular things between us because I was expressing more of my own anger to her. Things became more balanced as I came to terms with an aspect of my shadow, anger, and learned to communicate those feelings more effectively in our relationship.

The challenge of love is to accept the totality of your partner's shadow and light

Because of the complexity of our human nature, there are an endless number of possible disowned selves within us attempting to get our acceptance by using our relationships as mirrors. Here are just a few examples of possible polarities which may play out in your relationships:

Vulnerability and strength – The strong partner may judge the sensitivity of the vulnerable partner as being needy while the vulnerable partner may judge the power of the strong partner as dominating.

Materialistic and artistic – The materialistic partner may judge the creativity of the artistic partner as irresponsible while the artistic partner may judge the work ethic of the materialistic partner as greedy.

Energetic and relaxed – The energetic partner may judge the laid-back attitude of the relaxed partner as laziness while the relaxed partner may judge the vitality of the energetic partner as being too hyper.

Intellectual and emotional – The intellectual partner may judge the feelings of the emotional partner to be smothering while the emotional partner may judge the logic of the intellectual partner as being cold.

Organized and unstructured – The organized partner may judge the untidiness of the unstructured partner as being chaotic while the unstructured partner may judge the order of the organized partner to be overly rigid.

Extroverted and introverted – The extroverted partner may judge the quietness of the introverted partner as being antisocial while the introverted partner may judge the enthusiasm of the extroverted partner as being egotistical.

Promiscuous and prudish – The promiscuous partner may judge the conservativeness of the prudish partner as repressive while the prudish partner may judge the uninhibited passion of the promiscuous partner to be immoral.

We are often attracted to a partner who possesses opposite qualities from what we have developed within our own being. It's as if those opposite qualities complete us in some way. Unfortunately, the qualities that attract us to our partner initially are often the same qualities which later cause us trouble.

When we first meet, everything is okay because we are stretching toward our partner, wanting to be a little more like them. After a while, we start polarizing back to our respective corners because we're not used to expressing the unique qualities embodied by our partner.

The key to creating harmony is for both partners to reach out and strive to develop in themselves the opposite qualities seen within their partner that they were attracted to in the first place. As they do, balance is established in the relationship and each individual partner becomes more whole.

> The people we are in relationship with are always a mirror, reflecting our own beliefs, and simultaneously we are mirrors reflecting their beliefs. So relationship is one of the most powerful tools for growth. If we look honestly at our relationships we can see so much about how we created them.
>
> Shakti Gawain,
> American author, human potential teacher.

When you take responsibility for any denied parts of you within your relationships and fully accept them as your own, a healing takes place, communication is cleared and compassion blooms in your heart.

How to use the Mirroring Process

CAUTION: *At first the mirroring process can be difficult to grasp because humans are so used to looking for reasons outside of ourselves for the difficulties in our lives and then placing the blame on others. Learning to accept and reclaim the denied parts of your being will take time, so be patient. If you persevere in the process of looking for the gifts which your partner is reflecting to you, I assure you that your life will dramatically improve in all areas.*

Strong emotional reaction – If you have a strong emotional reaction to someone's behavior, then you are probably experiencing a reflection of one of the denied parts of yourself. With the shadow, you may find yourself both attracted to, and repelled by, that quality in the other person. Your emotional reactions serve as a diagnostic tool to inform you of a probable mirroring situation taking place with the other person.

Find the offensive trait in the other person – Now it's important for you to step away from your emotional reaction by becoming more mentally detached. By using your mind in a manner of objective observation, you are able to look for the specific offending trait or quality in the other person. Keep looking for the reason the individual affects you so strongly. A general statement like, "He makes me so angry," will not be specific enough. You must distill the various reasons for being upset down to one primary quality.

For example, you may be angry with someone because she is never direct with you and you often feel maneuvered and guilty when you're in her company. After you analyze it, you boil it down to her manipulation as the reason you were emotionally plugged in to her. So, the offending trait you were looking for was manipulation. Another example could be a friend who is never there for you when you need him. You're always helping him but he never has time for you. As you search for the upsetting quality in him, you discover that his actions are selfish. In this situation, the offending trait was his selfishness.

Look within yourself for the same trait – Now this is where it gets a little tricky, because of your natural resistance to accepting responsibility for the presence of a so-called negative trait within you. If you are brutally honest with yourself, and look deeply within, you will discover a time in your past when you have expressed the very same trait as the person you have the issue with. (Don't worry; quite often, the reflected trait will be greatly exaggerated in the person who offends you, in order to get your attention. It is as if the energy has to knock loudly on the door of your awareness in order for you to see your disowned voice within.) Remember this is a part of your shadow that you are completely denying so until you get the hang of it, finding the reflected trait in yourself takes concentration and a willingness to see the truth.

You may say, "There is no way I am anything like that manipulative jerk. I've searched high and low and I haven't seen any time in the past where I have been manipulative." And maybe you are right in that you haven't been manipulative for the past 20 years. In the distant past, you may have judged the manipulative part of you so harshly that you have completely avoided expressing it. Just because you haven't expressed it, doesn't mean it's not there. We have a natural tendency to forget our distasteful qualities. Maybe when you were a child you manipulated your father into giving you an extra scoop of ice cream with just a fluttering of your eyes and a sweet, "Please, Daddy, please?" Believe me, every child by the time of five years of age has developed advanced skills in the art of manipulation!

After finding the trait within, learn to accept it as a part of you – It's not enough to see the trait within you.

The next step is to fully allow it to be a part of your awareness by consciously accepting it as yours. Initially, this is not always easy because of your long-time negative judgment of this denied part of you.

You might as well learn to accept it because now that you have discovered its presence you can no longer stick your head in the sands of denial. You don't have to do anything with it other than just allow it to be included in the total you. Even if your acceptance is reluctant, integration will occur anyway if you can allow yourself to hold the tension of its presence within you.

If you can learn to see some of the positive aspects of the negative quality, it will help you to accept it. For instance, even though it's done in a covert way, the manipulative part of you is very good at getting your needs and desires met. Instead of manipulating circumstances behind the scenes, you can learn to use its creative energy to fulfil your desires by shifting to a more assertive approach of asking directly for what you want.

Another example would be learning to recognize the positive aspects of your anger. As you no longer judge your anger to be a destructive quality, you are able to assertively get what you want in the world because it gives you the power to make things happen. With your anger available to you, you can access the inner warrior in you when needed to protect you from emotional or physical harm. If you look closely, you will find shimmering jewels in the dark seeds of your shadow.

Acceptance stops negative mirroring – By finally accepting the previously rejected part of you, you'll no longer be negatively affected by the same trait in the person who originally upset you. The reason your higher self-created a mirror reflection of a quality in another person was to call your attention to a similar quality that was disowned in you. When you finally give your attention and acceptance to the unloved part of you, there will no longer be any need for the reflection. I've experienced it time and time again. I could have a longstanding problem with an individual, and as soon as I discovered and accepted the denied trait in me that the person was mirroring back, the person would no longer affect me in a negative way. It's magical the way this process occurs. So if you are trying to change someone (which is almost impossible to do), stop and instead change yourself by looking at what the reflection is trying to teach you and somehow, some way, the other person will shift without you saying a word.

Learn from the reflection and still maintain boundaries – There is a fine line between accepting a rejected quality as yours that is seen reflected in another person and allowing the other person's negative behavior to hurt you. After you have reclaimed your disowned quality, the offending trait may no longer emotionally affect you to the same degree.

However, sometimes the person may still continue the behavior which originally offended you. Even though you are now integrating the previously rejected quality, it's important to establish and maintain strong boundaries so as to protect yourself from harm.

Explain the effect of their behavior on you and give him or her a chance to change. If the person continues to offend you, you always have a choice to withdraw from the relationship.

Benefits of seeing your relationships as mirrors:

- Greater self-acceptance of your dark and light shadow qualities.
- Less judgmental of self and others.
- Increased compassion.
- Eliminates self-sabotage.
- Reduces inner stress.
- Less anger, more harmony.
- Abolishes the blaming of others.
- Eradicates gossip.
- Prevents the attraction of negative mirrors.

- Stops you from playing the victim game.
- Accepting responsibility makes you empowered. New creative energies are integrated into your life. Expanded sense of awareness of the total you.
- Greater vitality and emotional passion.
- Increased sense of safety within your relationship.
- Replacing blame with passion leads to sizzling sex.
- Spiritual wisdom grows – Know thyself.

One does not become enlightened by imagining figures of light, but by making the darkness conscious.

Carl G Jung, (1875 – 1961),
Swiss psychiatrist.

Chapter 10

Forgiving the Past

Forgiveness is the fragrance the violet sheds on the heel that has crushed it.
Mark Twain, (1835-1910),
American humorist, writer.

The message of this chapter is short and sweet: It's impossible to experience fulfillment in love while continuing to harbor resentments from the past.

It is not only the unhealed resentments with your partner that interfere with your ability to receive love. It's also the stockpiled anger towards other people who may have wronged you long ago which continues to disturb your present intimate relationship.

How can you fully love anyone as long as anger stagnates in your heart?

If you're holding on to hurts from the past, these lingering resentments will poison any prospects of a deeper intimacy with your partner in the present.

Learning to let go

As you begin to look for ways of releasing resentments from the past toward individuals who have hurt you, or learning to forgive yourself for any past pain you have caused to another, you'll encounter two opposite approaches to personal responsibility.

1. Accepting responsibility is when an individual

recognizes that their words or actions have caused pain to another. This individual then takes full responsibility for the action by sincerely apologizing to the person who was injured along with making a commitment not to do it again.

2. Denying responsibility is when an individual, for whatever reason, refuses to accept any responsibility for the negative impact of their words or actions on another. Because of the lack of sensitivity to the negative impact of their actions on another person, the individual may repeat their destructive behavior in the future.

Sometimes there's a variation of these two responses, when a person initially doesn't accept responsibility for hurting someone, but eventually awakens to the truth of the situation and chooses to come clean by accepting responsibility and apologizing.

Denying responsibility

If a person hurts you and refuses to accept any responsibility for their actions, it can be exceptionally difficult to let go of your anger and disappointment at their refusal to apologize.

If your partner has hurt you and continues to deny responsibility, then you have a real problem on your hands. There's a good chance your partner will repeat the action that hurt you and you could be at emotional risk. In other words, you won't feel safe.

Remember, part of taking care of yourself is learning to set appropriate boundaries with others. If your partner persists in hurting you without apologizing or changing their behavior then it's important for your emotional well-being to set stronger boundaries with your partner. Remember you always have a choice to leave an abusive situation.

The anger and disappointment at your partner's refusal to apologize and accept responsibility will accumulate with time. It's a situation that you will have to confront directly by strongly stating the limits of what you're willing to put up with, and if your limits are not honored then get out of the abusive relationship. Otherwise, your anger will build to the point where it will negatively affect your emotional and physical well-being.

Pain from the past

If someone deeply hurt you in the past, either physically, mentally or emotionally, and the wounds are still open because your offender never took responsibility for hurting you, you must come to a place of letting go of your resentment.

Holding on to resentments from the past are a huge obstacle to joy in your present life. You may say, "I can separate my past relationships from my current one. They're not the same, so why should I forgive someone who really hurt me." The reason you should consider letting go and forgiving the person who hurt you is that it's a burden to every aspect of your being. Your resentment weighs you down, affects your health and totally obstructs any possibility of true ecstasy in your present life.

A new approach to forgiveness

When I ask you to forgive someone, I'm not talking about a false type of forgiveness that just skims the surface. I'm talking about a much deeper, revolutionary type of forgiveness that recognizes that every situation that has occurred in your life, the good and the bad, the joyful and the sorrowful, has occurred because there was an opportunity for some kind of healing to take place.

A breakthrough book on releasing the past, called *Radical Forgiveness* by Colin C Tipping, clearly articulates the idea that there is a divine perfection in every situation and if we can rise to a higher vantage point, we can see the lessons learned from even our most difficult trials and tribulations.

At some point in your past, at least one individual who crossed your path has caused you pain. If you're honest with yourself, you will know that you have also consciously and unconsciously hurt someone in the past. It's part of the human condition. We are all learning how to balance ourselves physically, emotionally, mentally and spiritually and until we reach that balance we will occasionally become imbalanced in our reactions to others. It's our imbalance that impacts and affects other human beings in a negative way. Unless you're a perfectly balanced human being and you're sure that you have never hurt anyone else, get over your judgment of others because your judgment keeps you stuck in a state of being a victim.

When you let go of your anger and forgive someone for hurting you in the past, you free yourself from bondage to your personal history.

Forgiveness may not mean reconnecting

When you see how everything works out for the best, even the most painful previous experiences of your life, you can get to a place of finally releasing your judgments, pain and resentments. You can forgive yourself, the other person, and release your unwillingness to let it go.

Forgiving someone doesn't necessarily mean you have to feel renewed warmth, affection and love for them. You may actually experience apathy or a continued lack of respect for the person and yet you can still forgive. You can forgive by knowing that we learn lessons in every situation and some of our greatest growth occurs during times of friction and discord.

Because you're learning to set boundaries and protect yourself, forgiving a person who has harmed you does not mean that you have to re-associate, reconnect or ever socialize with them again. There's a good probability that they are still not safe to be with. If they haven't arrived at a place in life where they realized their mistake and tried to reach out to you to apologize, then it would probably be in your best interests to keep space between you.

On the other hand, quite often when you release your own resentment, forgive the past and see the greater gift or lesson in the past situation that hurt you, it opens a space for the other person to finally see the impact of their action and offer you their apology. At that point, if you feel safe, a new relationship can be formed where boundaries can be set up which enable you to re-establish your friendship on new ground.

Higher view

There's a perfection in this universe which draws experiences and people into our life to nudge and coerce us into new patterns of growth as human beings. Because of our general lack of awareness and overall resistance to change, many of these experiences are very painful at the time and most of them involve other people. On some higher soul level, we make an agreement with others to play out different situations with them for our mutual growth. Sometimes it is the very person we judge the most who may be providing us with the biggest lesson.

> Never be bullied into silence. Never allow yourself to be made a victim. Accept no one's definition of your life; define yourself.
> Harvey Fierstein, (1954 -),
> American actor, playwright.

It certainly doesn't feel that way when a difficult situation is being played out with another person. There's a lesson in everything— the good, the bad, the joyful and the sad. It's just that we don't usually discover the deeper meaning of most of the events occurring in our life at the time. Often, as the river of time creates distance from the event, we can look back and understand the full meaning and lessons learned. Long after a hurtful event in your life, how many times have you said, "I never thought I would one day be looking back and laughing at the situation because at the time I was devastated. Now I can see why it happened and I'm glad that it did because I'm a better person for it."?

Even if you can't see the lesson in a situation you're trying to forgive, believe me, there is one. So why continue to judge someone who may be assisting you in some convoluted way to become a more whole human being? Forgiving means knowing that there is some ultimate lesson that you needed to learn from the situation, however painful, and that it's now okay to let your pain go. If you trust that there was a benefit to you of some kind, it will be easier for you to release the past. Otherwise, your blame and resentment will disempower you by keeping you in your victimhood.

For some of you who have experienced tremendous pain, this can be a very difficult concept to get your head around because of the emotion attached. Perhaps someone emotionally or physically abused you. It can be exceptionally difficult to find any lesson learned from the experience. Maybe the lesson acquired was refusing to allow yourself to ever be involved in a similar situation again. From time to time we all fall over obstacles. What's important is to realize that even though we may have tripped and fallen, at least we have landed on the other side of the obstacle. We pick ourselves up and carry on with life, with the knowledge that we overcame the obstacle and know where it lies.

I'm not asking you to totally embrace this concept and believe it. What I am asking you to do is to sit with this idea for a while and test it out in your own life. Look back at some of the hurtful events of the past to see if there were any positive effects on your overall development. There is always light in the darkest of nights.

Revenge feeds resentment

We may refuse to forgive another because of our unconscious desire for revenge. We somehow feel that if we forgive someone, we will let the person off the hook. By holding onto anger, you think you are somehow balancing the scales and the person who hurt you will suffer because of it. The exact opposite is true. The only person who will be hurt by your resentment will be you. Resentment shortens your life span and definitely takes the fun out of life.

Let go of your resentment, forgive the person who hurt you and let Universal Law deliver its inevitable karmic lesson. The law of cause and effect rules this world with an iron fist. For every cause there is an effect, for every action, a reaction, and for every positive thought you plant, good will return to you multiplied. But when you sow the wind, you will reap the whirlwind. In other words, if you cause harm to another individual, whether it's emotional, physical, or mental, at some point in your life the negative karma you've created will rain down on you when you least expect it. You're free to forgive when you're not worried about revenge because the cosmic hit man of planet Earth called cause and effect is sure to take care of things for you.

> An eye for eye only ends up making the whole world blind.
> Mahatma Gandhi, (1869 – 1948),
> Indian political, spiritual leader.

Forgiveness leads to fulfillment

If you are harboring dark thoughts and feelings from your past, your ability to connect with another soul will be greatly restricted. The heart is like a container, a cup that retains the cumulative feelings of your life. If your cup is full of pain, resentment and blame, there is no room for joy, fulfillment and ecstasy.

By letting go of anger and disappointment from the relationships of your past, you free up a tremendous amount of emotional space in your heart to give and receive love more abundantly. You become lighter and lighter as you release those heavy emotions from your being and you start ascending toward the higher vibratory feelings such as ecstasy, union and ultimate fulfillment with your current partner.

It's hard work and it will take time but, believe me, the quest is well worth the effort.

Accepting Responsibility

If a person sees the harmful impact of their action on you and apologizes with a sincere sense of remorse, then you will feel a sense of relief. The residual pain that you feel because of their action may still sting a bit, but a sense of safety will be restored to your relationship because of their acceptance of responsibility. It's important at this point to begin to let go of your hurt and anger toward the person who caused you pain.

I can hear you say, "But Des, he hurt me so much that it seems impossible for me to let go of the pain. I can forgive but I can't forget." Maybe what you're really saying is, "I won't forgive and I won't forget." If you really forgive another, there is a peace that comes upon you.

Right now, just say these words and see how you feel, "I can forgive but I can't forget." It feels like you're still holding onto something, doesn't it? That's because you are. You're choosing to cling to your resentment.

Nobody ever forgets where he buried the hatchet.
Kin Hubbard, (1868 - 1930),
American humorist, journalist.

Often you will hold on to your anger in a self-righteous attitude which then communicates to the person who hurt you, "How dare you hurt me that way. Now I'm going to punish you for your transgression by withdrawing my love and not letting you off the hook."

Your resentments become leverage, which you can use to control that person by creating a sense of guilt. They're in your emotional debt and they owe you big-time. Your resentment will always be waiting for you, ready to use in your manipulative bag of tricks at the moment when you choose to drag up the past hurt as a tool to control your partner with guilt.

It's especially destructive to your relationship to do this when your partner has accepted responsibility and apologized for hurting you. Why won't you let it go?

If there is someone in your life who keeps bringing up a past hurt for which you offered an apology, and has a problem letting it go, ask them this question, "How much longer are you going to hold on to your anger toward me — one month, six months, 10 years?"

From my experience, you won't get an answer if they aren't willing to let it go. They'll just ignore you or change the subject, but they won't answer you. On the other hand, your question may assist them in finally looking at the absurdity of wasting their precious time by worrying about something from the past, and they may at last let go of their resentment.

Accepting apologies and moving on

When someone has hurt your feelings and caused you pain in some way, it is not easy to let go of your anger. It's natural to feel anger when someone wounds you, and that anger may stay around for a while, though it becomes deeply destructive when it hangs around for a long time. If a person understands that they may have offended you and offers you a heartfelt apology, then it's important to rise above your pain, allow the old wound to heal and start anew.

> The weak can never forgive.
> Forgiveness is the attribute of the strong.
> Mahatma Gandhi, (1869 – 1948),
> Indian political, spiritual leader.

It's inevitable in the course of an intimate relationship for you to step on each other's toes from time to time. As imperfect human beings learning to balance the complex emotional flow in partnerships, there will be many opportunities for you to say "sorry: to each other for actions which may have caused pain.

It takes great courage to look within yourself and take responsibility for any damage you may have caused another human being and say to them, "I'm sorry." If you want your partner to do the same for you then you better start taking emotional responsibility for your impact on them by courageously apologizing when your actions may have caused harm.

True forgiveness is the key

If your partner is truly sorry for an action that may have caused you pain, and requests your forgiveness, then it's vitally important for you to let go of your anger and resentment once and for all.

Dump it, get rid of it, burn it up, release it, throw it to the wind, shout it to the moon, vaporize it, eradicate it and just plain get over it, because it is slowly destroying any chance of fulfillment in your relationship. Whatever it takes for you to finally let go of your resentment – do it now.

Resentment Release Process

1. Make an appointment with yourself when you can have a quiet time to sit down and think about the people in your past that you have issues with which are unresolved. Search within to discover if there are any residual feelings of sorrow, anger or resentment toward someone from your past. Include your partner and your present life situation. As you discover these uncompleted emotional experiences, write them down on a pad of paper by listing the person's name, the reason or cause for your feelings and a description of those feelings such as anger, sorrow, or fear. Do this for every person in your past or present who may have hurt you and where the issue remains unresolved. (The process of expressing your feelings by the written word is almost magical in the way in which it assists you in dynamically releasing pent-up feelings and emotions in a most elegant way.)

2. Select one of the individuals on your list of resentments. Start with the person and the issue you feel most unresolved about and begin to write a letter to that person who hurt you. Pour your heart and soul into your writing because this letter is meant to be for your eyes only. This letter is not to be mailed. If you feel anger then

let it rip onto the page by being totally honest with your feelings. Don't hold back. As you allow yourself to express these long-held resentments, don't be surprised at the intensity of your feelings. Keep writing until you have nothing left to say. The key to this process is to freely allow whatever feelings you experience to flow through you unchecked. When you have completed, signed and dated your letter, get a pot or a bowl and go outdoors. Place the letter in the bowl and burn it to symbolically release your resentment.

3. After a few days, sit down and check-in to see if there are any additional feelings that you may need to express. Maybe in your inner search you won't find any more resentment. That's good because it means that you have let it go. Perhaps you may discover another layer of pain underneath the previous one. Just write another letter and allow any residual feelings to flow onto the page and repeat the process of burning the letter again.

4. Over the next several weeks, work through all of the resentments on your by list repeating the previous process. As you release your long-held anger and hurt, you will begin to feel a sense of emotional buoyancy in your heart.

5. It's not necessary to mail the letter to the person who harmed you because the healing is taking place within you, regardless of the other person's involvement or willingness to participate.

6. If, however, you feel that you would like to mail a letter to the person you were resentful toward, then do so but don't send the first draft, which is probably full of your anger. Keep writing until the bitterness in your pen is gone and then mail your letter. It's very important for you to release that letter with no expectation of how the other person will receive it. The person may or may not respond to your letter so let go of all attachment to any

particular result that you may desire. You have no control over another's reaction. The only control you have is over your capacity to see the higher good in the situation and to forgive and release the past. Your power lies in your ability to move on.

7. If the person is your partner, then choose the right time to sit with your partner and give them the incredible gift of your forgiveness. Let them know that you agree to release your resentment once and for all.

Offering the gift of apology

If you have hurt someone in the past and you haven't accepted responsibility for your words or actions which caused pain to them, then it's high time that you offered your sincere apology. It doesn't matter if the event took place a decade, a week, or an hour ago, because time is irrelevant when it comes to an act of love. Don't let the curtain of this lifetime descend before you make your amends. Clear things up before you or the other person departs from this world and you'll gratefully shed the heavy baggage of regrets.

Again, using the written word is a great way for you to get straight with the person you hurt by sitting down and writing a genuine apology for your hurtful act. Don't beat yourself up but be clear and specific about your need for an apology.

Believe me; it is well worth the effort because you will feel a wonderful sense of relief for finally balancing the scales of personal responsibility in your human interactions.

Eye to eye

If you feel safe, sit down with the person you offended, look them straight in the eye and tell them you are sorry. Your words of contrition will heal their hurt. Your courage to accept responsibility will be viewed by them as a very brave act.

> If we could read the secret history of our enemies, we would find in each person's life sorrow and suffering enough to disarm all hostility.
>
> Henry Wadsworth Longfellow, (1819 - 1892), American poet.

Forgiveness Agreement

As Intimate Partners,

we_____

and_____ agree to forgive each other for any hurt we may have caused in the past.

I agree:
- to fully forgive my partner for any prior offenses toward me.
- to let go of any resentments toward people from my past.
- to accept responsibility for any pain I may cause another and to apologise when necessary.
- to avoid revisiting any past transgressions of my partner.

_____   _____
        Partner   **Signatures**   Partner

_____   _____
         Date   Date

Chapter 11

No-No Land
Attractions & Affairs,
the Ultimate Taboo

There are few things that we so unwillingly give up, even in advanced age, as the supposition that we still have the power of ingratiating ourselves with the opposite sex.
Samuel Johnson, (1709 - 1784),
British author.

Love affairs and deceptions create more damage and pain than any other single area of our relationships.

On the other hand, an affair sometimes occurs as a catalyst to move us out of a hopeless relationship that we stubbornly refuse to leave.

If in the past you have had affairs, then the last thing you need to do is to judge yourself harshly while reading this chapter. Please refrain from creating any more guilt than you may already have. Gaining insights and learning from your past is the goal.

I have been on both sides of the fence. I have initiated affairs at a partner's expense and partners have had affairs on me. I can assure you that neither side of the fence is any fun.

When I was the one who was doing the betraying, the pleasure and excitement derived from the experience was not equal to the massive pain, guilt and lowered self-esteem that resulted from my choice. When I was the one who was betrayed, the deep sense of abandonment, loss and total shock was intensely overwhelming. Either way I know how you feel.

My intention in writing this chapter is to support you in avoiding the dangers and pitfalls of external love affairs because in my life they have caused others and myself unnecessary pain.

You can't guarantee fidelity

No matter how you may feel about this, you can't predict whether or not you will have an affair. The more self-righteous you become about it, the more likely you are to have an affair.

I can hear you saying, "I don't care what you say. I know I would never have an affair. I'm just not like that." Be careful with such absolute pronouncements because I once claimed the same high moral ground as you and when I fell, I fell hard.

At the very best, we can set up a strong intention to remain faithful. A strong positive statement could be, "I fully intend, with the assistance of the Great Spirit, to stay sexually and emotionally faithful to my partner when a moment of choice arises in my life."

All life choices are acted out moment by moment.

I strongly believe that if you're at the point where you're going to initiate an affair, or already have one cooking, then either fix the relationship with your partner or get the hell out. You owe it to yourself and to your partner.

What comes around goes around

If the former paragraph upsets you and you don't have the will, integrity or courage to accept responsibility for your actions, then look at it from a purely practical point of view.

There is a law of cause and effect working in this universe.

This means that our thoughts and actions, whether positive or negative, create effects that will someday be returned to us. How else could we learn? Therefore, if we cause harm to others by our selfishness, insensitivity, or deception, then one day in the future when you least expect it someone will return the deception to you.

Believe me, I know. I learned the hard way. You never get away with it.

At the start of the 21st century, as women with their newfound freedoms and financial independence are starting to rival men in having affairs, there is probably more sleeping around than ever before on this hot-blooded planet.

It doesn't matter if the whole human herd is going down that path because you are an individual with a will and a mind of your own, fully capable of choosing truth, avoiding deception, and creating your own path of honesty.

Why is this happening?

Denial of lust is the core of the problem

Humans are incredibly complex beings, with very opposite sub-personalities within us that compete for dominance, as mentioned before in Chapter 9, My Partner, My Mirror. There is a part of us that is loyal and there is an opposite part of us that could betray another in a blink of an eye.

Whatever we suppress will someday, in some way, be expressed in our outer world. Even the most despicable and loathsome parts of our nature want to be included in our consciousness. One of the parts of us that has been denied and suppressed more than any other is the indulgent, free-spirited, and lustful part of our personality.

We know this part of us is hiding within, yet we act as if it isn't there. These inner qualities are capable of fantasizing about, and sometimes pushing us to directly experience, attractions to others. This can result in an actual affair which is mental, emotional or physical in form.

"You have nothing to worry about, dear; I have eyes only for you. It could never happen. I couldn't possibly have an affair."

At the moment of making that statement, the part of you that is totally committed to your partner believes it to be true and to that loyal part within you, it is true.

Have you ever noticed that the moment you identify with one part of yourself, in this case the super committed part of you that says, "I will never betray you," the exact opposite energy arises within? It may say, "Oh yeah, so you think you couldn't possibly have an affair? Deal with this attraction then!" Soon your inner free spirit pulls an attraction toward you.

Perhaps this has never happened to you, but for many of us attractions to people outside of our primary relationship are going to occur from time to time. Sometimes these attractions can be overwhelming.

Our traditional culture, for the sake of protecting the unity of the family, has fostered the idea that when you're in love you should never experience attractions to others. If we do experience them, we should deny those urges and impulses.

In other words, you are pressured by these unspoken rules to suppress the part of yourself that couldn't care less about being loyal to your partner, the free spirit part of you that wants to experience the interaction and complexity of multiple relationships. When this happens, strong inner currents and tensions are formed which demand huge reserves of emotional energy to suppress your lustful nature. Sometimes these primal energies overwhelm your ability to keep them repressed and they burst forth in the form of a love affair that excludes your partner.

Truth is the key to prevention

When an affair occurs, it is usually the final manifestation of a series of events that have taken place within the relationship. However, we focus on this culminant event as the reason the relationship is in trouble or may possibly end.

Actually, it's the minor withholds that accumulate over time which erode the energetic connection in the relationship. When the daily aggravations and myriad stresses which arise between couples aren't communicated in an effective way, tensions build that are destructive to the relationship.

It's usually at this time that we unconsciously create emotional distance from our partner. This is when we are most vulnerable to other romantic possibilities. The grass starts looking very green on the other side of the hill.

Secret love affairs become public love affairs

Secret love affairs inevitably become public love affairs. Even if you're in that small percentage of people who are never discovered and you pride yourself on your ability to keep your affair secret, you're totally deluding yourself. If you say to yourself, "What they don't know won't hurt," you're wrong.

What they don't know will hurt

Even if your partner never finds out about your affair, the very fact that you're withholding such a time bomb of deception creates a deep psychic rift in the relationship, which slowly bleeds the union to the death. Even though you think that you're getting away with it, your conscience, your higher self, starts needling you with guilt. You go home to your partner carrying with you a dark secret that weighs on your soul. No matter how much you try to run away from your actions, you can't escape. The next time you are with your partner, you will not be able to communicate with them from your wholeness because parts of you that are in deception are preventing you from being in your truth.

The most vulnerable part of your partner, their inner child, unconsciously senses that deception is in the air and begins to emotionally withdraw from the relationship. Consciously they may not know that you are playing around. On some level, it just doesn't feel safe to them.

If you are the partner that's being betrayed, it's especially disconcerting when the betraying partner continually lies to you in order to cover up the deception. Even if you sense some hanky-panky going on behind your back, you desperately want to believe your partner because the alternative would be devastating. So you ignore your intuitive cues and keep hoping for the best.

Usually the affair eventually erupts into the open and the pain experienced by both is the most intensely raw, overwhelming and devastating of human emotions that can be experienced. When the person that you're supposedly closest to betrays the bonds of trust, a deep sense of abandonment can linger for a long time.

When an affair occurs it is very difficult to reestablish the bonds of trust that have been ruptured by the deception. It can be done and yet it will take time and a mutual rededication to valuing truth and commitment as the cornerstone of your relationship. Reaching out for professional counseling support can be vital to assisting you in rooting out underlying causes and getting you both back on track. It's hard work but it can be done.

Emotional affairs

For the most part, when an affair occurs, most of us focus on the sexual betrayal as the big issue. And yet most physical affairs begin with a connection on an emotional, feeling level between individuals. In fact, many people would be more upset if their partner had a strong emotional link to the person they were having the affair with. It's one thing for two people to do a purely physical, sexual act. However, if there is connection established between them which includes intimacy and affection, the destructive impact to the primary relationship can be increased dramatically.

A good percentage of emotional affairs spiral into a physical one. However, if it remains emotional without the physical element, it's easy to delude yourself into thinking that you're not doing anything wrong because it's not sexual. It is, however, negatively impacting your relationship with your partner because of your attachment to someone else emotionally. We have only so much emotional energy to go around. So if we're directing our attention away from our partner to someone outside of our primary relationship, then that leaves a lot less for you and your partner. You will also put less effort into working things out in your own relationship because it seems so easy to get your emotional nurturing from somewhere else.

> There's so many different ways to cheat. People think infidelity is the way to cheat. I think it's sometimes far worse to emotionally cheat on somebody.
> Sandra Bullock American (1964-)
> Actress/Producer

If a sexual affair is considered a major breach of trust in the relationship, why wouldn't an emotional affair be any different?

If you're going through problems at home with your partner, it can feel good confiding in someone else who seems to understand you. And yet, revealing confidentialities and intimacies to someone else about your own personal relationship is actually a betrayal of the trust between you and your partner.

A good test to determine whether or not you're in an emotional affair is your willingness to reveal to your partner everything that you shared with the other person. If you are in an emotional affair, the chances are slim that you will want to reveal anything to your partner about it and that's where the danger arises.

It's the secrecy which adds to the excitement, and the quickest way to diffuse the danger of you pulling away from your partner and toward the new person is to reveal to your partner the attraction that you are experiencing. Once the mystery is pierced, often the attraction level is also reduced in intensity.

Social Media

With the advent of social media, re-connections with others from the past who normally would not have crossed your path again are occurring more and more often. It's easy to get lost in the illusions of the past and get caught up in an emotional infidelity. Private messaging often creates a false sense of quick intimacy which may lead one to share personal information with someone outside of your relationship.

It's important not to keep secrets from your partner when it comes to who is contacting you from the past. If a lover from the past contacts you on social media and wants to reestablish a connection, then it's important to tell your partner about it sooner rather than later. By revealing the truth about the past connection, you build deeper levels of trust with your partner and you keep the attention and energy focused on your primary relationship.

The best antidote to getting caught up in a social media affair is to pierce the cloak of secrecy by being fully open with your partner. If you would feel totally okay with allowing your partner to read any of your texts or social media messages, then you are most probably not anywhere close to an emotional affair. On the other hand, if you would not want to reveal to your partner the contents of any correspondences such as texts or emails, then you may be headed for the slippery slope of an emotional affair or you are already participating in one. In that event, it's important to ask yourself the question, are you moving away from your partner and toward the new person?

Prevention is easier

Your best insurance against deceptive affairs is to share your deepest personal truth with each other, and to clear the air of any resentments and withholds that may be stored.

Using the Talking Stick to continually clear any withholds between you helps to keep a strong connection on a feeling level. Quite often, this alone will prevent you from drifting apart and being attracted to any green grass on other hills.

Redirecting the energy of attractions

Another measure to prevent affairs from developing is to use the power of your outside attractions as an aphrodisiac for your own relationship.

If you have developed strong bonds of trust in your relationship, then learning how to do this is easier than you think. It's just that we are so used to hiding any flirtations we may have from our partner, we think if we speak the truth about them we are going to get into big trouble!

> To have a man who can flirt is the next thing to indispensable to a leader of society.
> Margaret Oliphant, (1828 - 1897),
> British novelist, historian.

Human beings are attracted to beauty in any form whether it is in a flower, a sunset, or in the eyes of another human. It's as natural as breathing and beauty brings joy to the senses while filling the heart.

When we appreciate the exquisite beauty of an orchid in our garden, does it mean that we must turn our eyes away from the rose next door? In seeing a beautiful sunset, does the sunset demand that we not look with delight upon the rising moon?

We humans are a funny breed in that we allow ourselves to appreciate all beauty wherever it is found, unless of course we are in an intimate relationship. Because of our personal insecurities, we feel too threatened to allow our partner to appreciate the beauty in another person.

Appreciating the beauty of others is as natural as breathing

I realize that sharing your attractions with your partner is a radical concept for most people to accept and understand because it seems counterintuitive. Many individuals fear that if their partner finds out about their attraction to someone else, it will hurt the relationship and not help it. Others may say that they rarely or never have attractions to others. For those individuals, the concepts that follow will not be of practical use to them. And yet it's safe to say that most people will have attractions to others from time to time. So I suggest that you stretch your mental comfort zone by opening up to the possibility that sharing attractions with each other can actually bring you closer together and add some spice to your relationship.

We all flirt

When we are in an intimate relationship, it's an unspoken rule that we don't give and receive flirtatious attention to other people. Therefore, we go underground and hide our attractions from each other. But who's kidding who? From time to time, we all sneak a peek! When we keep it from our partner, we not only degrade the trust level of our relationship by withholding our truth but we miss out on the positive aspects of outside attractions.

Sharing attractions stimulates passion

By sharing our attractions with our partner, we strengthen the bonds of trust and we redirect the energy from the attraction back into our relationship.

I remember a time when my former lover, Rebecca, taught me a valuable lesson in attractions. We were at a party when a friend of Rebecca came up to us and started talking to her. As they were in a humorous conversation, my attention was distracted toward a table of food where a very attractive woman in a red dress was bending over and reaching for some hors d'oeuvres. My attention was transfixed on the shape of her thoroughbred derriere when a tap on my shoulder disturbed my momentary pleasure.

Rebecca asked, "Do you like what you are looking at?" "What you talking about? I was looking at the dip," I responded. "Get real," Rebecca exclaimed. Realizing that I was seriously busted, I quickly attempted a retreat.

"Well now that you mention it, I did notice her quite attractive red dress," I offered.

Rebecca wouldn't let it go as she said, "Come on Des, if you can't be truthful with me about the small things how can you ever be truthful about bigger issues."

What could I say? She was right and I was also feeling increasingly embarrassed by my deception so, expecting the worst, I came clean.

"Okay you're right. I was looking at her rear end but it wasn't anywhere near as firm as yours, dear," I confessed, expecting her temper to erupt at any moment.

Instead, she said, "Thanks for telling the truth because it's totally understandable why you were attracted to her. She's a beautiful woman. Des, it's inevitable that you and I are going to have attractions to other people from time to time, so why don't we allow each other the space to feel someone else's appreciation of us. If we can do this then we can take the energy generated from the attraction back into our relationship and keep it all for ourselves. If we trust each other then everything should be okay." This is the last thing I expected Rebecca to ever say but I was intrigued by her proposal so we decided to try it out for the rest of the party.

For me, the highest level of sexual excitement is in a monogamous relationship.
Warren Beatty, (1937 -),
American actor, director, producer, screenwriter.

We danced for a while and then I left Rebecca to get us something else to drink. At the bar, I struck up a conversation with a friend. After a while, I left him to return to Rebecca with our drinks but she was nowhere to be found. I looked around and saw her standing on the patio in close conversation with a suave Frenchman we had briefly met earlier in the evening.

He was all over her. She looked as if she were enjoying herself a little too much. I started to walk toward them with increasing levels of jealousy pumping through my veins, but remembered our earlier agreement to allow ourselves to flirt, so I just patiently stood there with two drinks in my hands. I couldn't help but watch my fiancée being hit on by this sleazy predator. Rebecca was looking increasingly animated and I wasn't sure how much longer I could deal with this situation.

I wanted to strangle him and started moving toward them again. My anger was rising with every step when Rebecca caught my eye and tugged on her right ear, which was our signal that everything is okay and to give her a little more space. I reluctantly stopped to give her a few more minutes of play. She quickly ended her conversation and returned to my side. Before I could tear into her, she said she admired my courage for giving her the freedom she wanted to enjoy her attraction and that she felt closer to me because she was turned on by my confidence. Little did she know how close I came to making a complete fool of myself. On the ride home, Rebecca acknowledged that she thought he was a handsome and charming man and that she appreciated the attention. She also said that she felt he was a little boy emotionally and it made her appreciate my strength and maturity.

Because of the lady in red and the Frenchman, that night Rebecca and I had the best lovemaking of our relationship. I remember thinking, "I like this game!"

How to handle attractions

Acknowledge and accept the attraction – There is no need to feel awful or to apologize to your partner for something that is completely natural. Attractions just happen. They're a force of nature and they only become problematic when they're denied and repressed.

Avoid denying feelings of attraction – We are taught to deny and repress certain feelings. We sometimes fear these energies because we think that if we allow ourselves to feel them, we may lose control and succumb to their power.

In fact, you're more inclined to lose control in some future attraction if you continually deny that these primal forces exist within.

Feel the attraction fully – Trust yourself in allowing the full energy of the attraction to be felt in your body. It can be a bit tricky to balance the feelings brought up by the attraction and the awareness that it is just an attraction and that you will not allow it to interfere or damage your primary relationship. If you're not used to playing with these very dynamic energies, then you must be careful that your fantasies don't override your common sense.

Share the attraction with your partner – It won't feel natural at first. Can you imagine coming home from work tomorrow and saying, "My darling I wanted to share with you that I experienced a strong attraction to the boss's secretary today!" On the other hand, how about, "Welcome home dear. The repairman fixed the television today and I noticed when he left that I felt all tingly inside!" Somehow, it just doesn't feel right and yet when we start exercising this new muscle of truth, a whole new level of trust begins to develop in the relationship. If you are sharing an attraction with your partner, it's natural to experience some concern about the way he or she will receive it when you first begin to experiment with this process.

If you are receiving the sharing from your partner, expect to feel the various levels of jealousy that come up from time to time.

Sharing the attraction reduces its power – When an attraction is communicated to your partner; there is an immediate reduction in the mystery and pull of the attraction. It just seems to diminish over time.

Being non-judgmental encourages the truth – It's natural to experience jealousy listening to your partner reveal their attractions. It's important to understand that you would never have even been aware of the attraction if your partner didn't have the courage and integrity to tell you about it. Allow yourself to feel your jealousy. Just don't beat your partner over the head with it. After all, your partner loves you enough to tell you.

Build trust by revealing your attractions – If you can trust that your partner has the integrity and intention to inform you of their attractions, in time you will begin to feel safer and certain that there isn't any hanky-panky going on.

Create a Richter Scale of attraction – It's important to determine the strength of the attraction by some form of measurement. In one of my former relationships, my partner was a dynamic and beautiful woman who certainly experienced her share of admirers on a regular basis.

Occasionally, even I would have some crumbs of attention thrown my way! In order to keep our relationship safe and truthful we had developed the following scale that worked very effectively for us.

At any time either one of us could ask each other the question, "Have you had any attractions today, dear?" If we answered no then that's as far as it goes. If we answered yes then we may ask the other, "And what level was that attraction?" At that point we answered with a number that represented a level which reflected the intensity of the attraction. (This scale is open to your personal revision at any time. Make it work for you.)

Description of attraction:
Level number

1 – "Now that's a beautiful soul."
This is just a lighthearted appreciation of another fellow being. It is an admiration of someone's style, clothing, looks or smile.

2 – "Now that's a beautiful soul and check out that body."

We have now moved up a notch to the "turn your head around" stage where we may experience a relatively strong attraction to a person but it's only one sided. We appreciate their beauty.

3 – What you're attracted to is also attracted to you.

At this stage you and the person you are attracted to are experiencing an attraction to each other. It's definitely a stronger attraction and it's still safe as long as you don't put yourselves in situations where the attraction could grow to Level 4. For example, working late together at the office or meeting for business lunches on a regular basis could increase the intensity of the attraction, although usually, if shared with your partner, these Level 3 attractions are relatively harmless and can bring zest and energy into your relationship. A typical Level 3 is known as a flirtation. It feels good to be occasionally appreciated by someone other than your partner.

4 – "Darling, there is someone in the office that I'm strongly pulled towards, especially after I brushed up against her left breast at the water cooler." *("Houston, we have a problem!")*

Now we're in dangerous waters and it would be very easy to trip up and slide into the dreaded Level 5. An emotional affair has probably developed by this time. It is now extremely important that you tell your partner the truth about this Level 4 attraction because by doing so, you can reduce the intensity of the attraction. If you're not feeling safe with your partner's Level 4 attraction, then it's important that you each have what's called veto power. You can exercise that veto by demanding that your partner cut off the flirtatious connection completely. From my previous experience, Level 4s are not usually well received by your partner so you will probably need The Talking Stick for your own protection.

5 – "I've already been there."

This is where a person has actually crossed the line of physical infidelity. Needless to say, I'd be in big trouble if I told my partner that I had a Level 5 experience. It's just here for relevance purposes (and with the Great Spirit's help, may we never go to Level 5).

We find that by using this scale or one of your own, you and your partner can create a space of safety where you can allow the free spirit part of you to exist within your relationship without letting it get out of hand.

Sharing attractions reduces jealousy – By expressing the level of attraction you experience, your partner will feel safer knowing the degree of feeling you have for the other person. This eradicates unnecessary jealousy your partner may have from misinterpreting the strength of your attraction.

Jealousy can be an overwhelming emotion. It can humble the strongest souls. In our culture, jealousy has a bad reputation so we learned to suppress it. In fact, it's one of the most repressed emotions of our nature. Jealousy grows in the soils of denial, fear and insecurity. However, it's perfectly natural to feel jealousy from time to time. Sometimes, jealousy informs us that an actual attraction is taking place.

The best way to reduce your level of jealousy is to fully acknowledge that there is a part of you which can be jealous. Give yourself the space to allow your jealousy to express itself occasionally by sharing it with your partner and you'll prevent any overwhelming eruptions of jealousy from ruining your day. By sharing your attractions with each other, you both will begin to build strong trust levels because you are freely telling the truth. As trust builds, jealousy begins to diminish.

When your partner tells you about an attraction, it will still sting a bit but you will be able to quickly move through that initial twang of jealousy and you will begin to feel more secure. Because of our insecurities, we sometimes believe that something is wrong in our relationship or our partner may love us less if they are attracted to another person when in actuality it's just the harmless appreciation of the beauty of another being. Once you begin to understand that your partner's attraction to another individual has nothing to do with you, you will gradually build strong bridges of trust. Bringing your attractions to light creates the exact opposite effect from what you might expect. If you know and trust that your partner is going to reveal all their attractions to you, then you can relax your guard because of your increased level of security.

Let's be honest about it. Having all the jealousy in the world is not going to stop your partner from having an affair. The only safe protection you have is a strong sense of faith and trust in each other's integrity. If your partner is open and has the character to reveal to you the attractions to others of which you were unaware, then it's doubtful that you would be deceived by a full-fledged affair. If you're in the habit of keeping your physical attractions to others secret, you're much more likely to jump the fence when tempted.

Shared attractions revitalize sexuality. The vitality and energy generated by attractions can now be brought into your primary relationship and used as an aphrodisiac when safely shared with your partner.

CAUTIONS

Secrecy breeds desire, illusion and deception – If you're still tempted to withhold knowledge of your attraction from your partner, understand that you're playing with fire because keeping it secret usually increases the level of attraction. Because the attraction is hidden, fantasy and illusion come into play and the forbidden fruit starts looking very sweet. No matter what, tell your partner the truth as soon as possible.

If your relationship is in trouble, don't flirt – Have you ever noticed that strong attractions quite often show up when you and your partner are having problems in your relationship? At those times of stress and not feeling appreciated by your partner, the attention from an outside attraction appears to be particularly appetizing and tempting.

"Well, if my husband won't appreciate me, then I know someone who will." It's best to totally refrain from outside attractions until you and your partner have worked out your differences and are on safer ground.

Never embarrass your partner – It's important not to let the strength of an attraction cause you to do foolish things in public.

Falling out of a chair as a babe walks by your table or telling your man that you're attracted to the lifeguard's washboard stomach when your partner's tummy looks as if it's ready to give birth qualify as two good examples of what not to do. Always remember to choose the safety of the relationship over any possible attraction.

Consider the third party's feelings – Never encourage another person who wants more from you than you're willing to give them. Even though you are only feeling a lighthearted appreciation, the other person may have stronger feelings for you, so be careful.

> Why does a man take it for granted that a girl who flirts with him wants him to kiss her - when, nine times out of ten, she only wants him to want to kiss her?
> Helen Rowland, (1875 - 1950),
> American journalist.

Beware of predators – There are some men and women whose favorite sport is to intentionally disrupt happy relationships by aggressively seducing one of the partners in the relationship. Sounds unbelievable, but believe me, they exist. It's sort of like vampires. Nobody believes they really exist until one bites you on the neck.

The more committed the couple, the more challenged the

predator becomes in the pursuit of the partner. Usually predator types are single and when they have you in their sights, they can be devastatingly charming and almost irresistible. This is a Level 4 with teeth and the only antidote is the immediate clear and constant communication of this attraction to your partner and stepping away from this risky situation.

Expand your views

I realize that the ideas in this chapter may be provocative to some individuals but ignoring the truth about attractions will not make them go away. The alternative of not sharing your attractions is to lie to your partner about them, as many people do, and lying erodes trust. If you and your partner can stretch a bit by sharing the truth with each other about your personal attractions instead of denying the obvious, with a little practice you'll be pleasantly surprised by the invigorating energies rechanneled into your relationship.

CAUTION: Affairs need not always result in a negative outcome. If either of you has had an affair which came to light, there is no doubt that it was a major crisis point of your relationship. The accumulation of long held withholds is usually released all at once in a torrent of emotional discharge which can be overwhelming for each of you. It's true that many relationships can't withstand the storm of deception but it's also true that many unions are able to re-establish a strong foundation of love over time.

Sometimes an affair can serve as a catalyst that moves a couple from disengagement and apathy to communication and attention. Emotional energies are often liberated that can regenerate a deeper appreciation for each other. Often trust levels can be reestablished stronger than ever if both partners are willing to open their hearts to the purifying power of truth, compassion, and non-judgment.

I'm not advocating infidelities. I'm just saying that all is not lost if an affair occurs with someone outside of your relationship. If both you and your partner are willing to move to a deeper level of honesty and communication with each other than ever before, then a mutual commitment to your life together could transform a potential disaster into a renewal of your relationship.

Chapter 12

Women and Men - Two Peas in a Human Pod

The nearer society approaches to divine order, the less separation will there be in the characters, duties, and pursuits of men and women. Women will not become less gentle and graceful, but men will become more so. Women will not neglect the care and education of their children, but men will find themselves ennobled and refined by sharing those duties with them; and will receive, in return, co-operation and sympathy in the discharge of various other duties, now deemed inappropriate to women. The more women become rational companions, partners in business and in thought, as well as in affection and amusement, the more highly will men appreciate home.
Lydia M Child, (1802 - 1880),
American abolitionist, writer, editor.

The battle of the sexes, the longest running soap opera in the history of the planet, has been taking place for about 6000 years. This war suddenly transformed into a revolution of the sexes about 150 years ago. My fellow men, I highly advise you to get yourself a piece of white cloth, make it into a flag, and start waving it frantically, because the women are winning.

Don't worry, after their coming victory women won't rape and pillage as we males did centuries ago, but they will offer to share power in true partnership with men and lead the planet back into wholeness.

I can hear some of you say, "What revolution? I don't see any great change." It may not be obvious to you yet, but it's happening. The seeds for this revolution were planted sometime in the beginning of the 1800s. Since then those seeds have taken root in the soil of human interaction and are about to blossom into a revelation of true equality between men and women.

There has never been a greater opportunity for men and women to finally end our war of gender once and for all, by accepting the gifts that each has to offer. A century ago, things were very different, so let's look at the sequence of events which led us to the doorway of a golden era between the sexes. Taking a look at the last 200 years will assist you in gaining perspective on the massive changes which occurred between men and women and how those changes shaped today's relationships.

Trails from the past

Long ago, the difficult physical requirements of survival on planet Earth demanded that each gender needed to move into the function best suited for continued existence. Men and women polarized into their particular roles. The male, being the physically stronger of the two, was required to protect his family unit by going away to war, hunting for food and building suitable shelter. He couldn't run to the local supermarket for the night's meal. He had to go out to find food, kill it, and drag it home to his hungry family.

The female developed her nurturing capacity in order to take care of the children in the home environment while her man was away. She didn't have a microwave or running water in the hut. She often had to walk a mile or so to fill her animal skin with water at the local stream. She also got stuck with making the clothes, nurturing the kids and preparing food. He needed every ounce of his strength and courage.

She needed every bit of her love and patience. He was usually scared and she was usually bored. (What else is new?)

Men and women developed opposing strengths and weaknesses in their natures. Each developed qualities the other needed. They became totally dependent on each other. The man, with his superior physical abilities, provided the woman with shelter, a food source and protection against danger. The woman, with her superior nurturing skills, provided the man with emotional warmth, child rearing and sexual pleasure.

Adam said to Eve, "I was here first!"

Over time, men learned to value their dominant qualities of aggression and power while rejecting the feminine qualities of feeling, nurturing and sensuality. Patriarchy, or male domination, has ruled the planet for eons. The feminine aspects of the human race were regarded as inferior and were repressed.

Everything male was elevated and everything female was dominated. Religions were created which became exclusive clubs with only male gods and male priests allowed entrance. Spiritual books from every male-dominated religion were written in support of the patriarchy, denouncing women as being lesser creatures subservient to the whims of man.

As long as men controlled positions of authority in politics, religion, education, finances and family, women had no choice but to give in, hide their power, shut up and go along with the program. The few that had the courage to challenge male authority, like Joan of Arc... well, you know the story.

It's called History not Herstory

No wonder women are a bit upset with the old boys' club on planet Earth. We men had a good run but we should now lower the drawbridge, fill up the moat and let the women in before they storm the castle. It's high time we share the throne.

Women who experienced the dark side of male energy — dominating, brutal, greedy and egotistical — learned to judge and reject these same male qualities within themselves as destructive.

Men who experienced much of the dark side of female energy —manipulative, seductive, over-emotional and weak — learned to judge and reject these same female qualities within themselves as destructive.

"You can't live with them, and you can't live without them"

Remembering the mirroring process, whatever qualities we repress and judge within ourselves, when we see those same qualities reflected in another person we will judge and reject in them. Simultaneously, we are mysteriously attracted to the very people we judge because our consciousness is always seeking wholeness.

Men suppressed and denied their inner feminine qualities and needed the women in their lives to be responsible for their feelings and nurturing. Women suppressed and denied their inner male qualities and depended on men to physically protect and provide sustenance for them

Men and women needed each other to supply the qualities which were missing from their character. At the same time, they also resented having to depend on each other for these qualities.

> Every theory of love, from Plato down teaches that each individual loves in the other sex what he lacks in himself.
> G. Stanley Hall, (1844 - 1924),
> American psychologist, educator.

Women and men have had a love/hate relationship going on for a long, long time. There has been so much misunderstanding between the sexes that you would think men and women originate from different planets, yet they're genetically identical with just a few chromosomes tossed around here and there for spice.

Gender is balanced in nature

Observe nature and you will notice two sexes in everything which exists. In this world, gender expresses itself by way of opposites. Male and female are represented in animals, insects, and humans. On the atomic level gender is represented in opposite but complementary qualities. The structure of the atom is polarized into the proton and the electron which correspond to the masculine and feminine principle. A magnet is divided into the positive and negative poles. The Earth has the North and South Pole. If the universe is structurally wired with the male and female energies in balance then why shouldn't the human mind be balanced with equal polarities? It's in the mind where the imbalance has taken place because everything male has been elevated at the expense of everything female. The differences between men and women are more perceptual than actual. Yes it is true that there are major hormonal differences between the sexes but even with those chemical distinctions there are infinitely more similarities between men and women than differences.

The so-called battle of the sexes has been raging for thousands of years. Many people believe there is an inherent friction between the sexes which will cause this battle to be raged indefinitely. Countless people have focused attention on the differences rather than highlighting the similarities. Many books have been written explaining the battlefield tactics of the enemy, the opposite sex. These books clearly define the complexities and strange inner workings of the two genders, cleverly giving us the manipulative tricks needed to safely navigate the minefields of emotion, hidden and waiting in the other half. These books were helpful in their day and would continue to be so if it were not for the fact that the war between the sexes officially ended sometime around the year 1850. No one told them that the war ended, so they continue to promote the outdated concept that men and women are fundamentally different.

The Industrial Revolution liberated humanity from constrictive roles of gender

Mankind kept chugging along for millennia with women and men remaining polarized in their respective corners of total male and total female. Then along came a watershed event called the Industrial Revolution which changed everything.

The Industrial Revolution was at full steam around the mid-1800s and, for the first time in recorded history, mankind was liberated from the physical toils of day-to-day life. As farming, manufacturing and the home became increasingly mechanized, men and women benefited from the growing amount of leisure time. The pressure of physical survival lifted considerably, allowing people more time to spend in developing the mind.

A mental renaissance occurred which produced an original vision of women and men moving into areas of greater cooperation and equality. The practical idealism of Thomas Jefferson, Sojourner Truth and Mary Wollstonecraft brought the concepts of human rights, the abolition of slavery, and women's rights to the forefront of mankind's thinking. With the advent of the Industrial Revolution, across the globe democratic republics began to increase while autocratic dictatorships and crowned heads of state began to decline.

The 19th century produced some of mankind's greatest visionaries. Ralph Waldo Emerson, Harriet Martineau, John Stuart Mill and Elizabeth Cady Stanton were farsighted writers who clearly articulated a new way of expressing the masculine and feminine parts of our nature.

The development and distribution of electricity, along with breakthroughs in modes of transportation such as the train and eventually the motorcar, enabled unprecedented freedom to expand into totally new areas of living. A mass migration into the cities occurred and this new urbanization allowed men and women to interact in socially innovative ways.

Coeducation was a giant leap forward in the harmonization of roles between men and women, because it allowed them the opportunity to intermingle and learn from each other in a nonsexual way. When given the opportunity to study, women around the world excelled in the classroom and demonstrated beyond the shadow of a doubt that they were intellectual equals to men

Women's liberation led to men's liberation

The women's suffrage movement took root in the mid-19th-century and quickly swept the planet like wildfire. New Zealand became the first nation state in 1893 to give women the right to vote. Australia quickly followed in 1902. Because of strong religious opposition, the United States of America was one of the last western countries to enfranchise women, with an amendment to the Constitution allowing women the right to vote in 1920.

City life enabled women to participate in the workforce in ever-increasing ways. Women began to spread their wings by expressing themselves in positions of employment which earlier had been the domain of men. Once women tasted freedom of expression and were no longer relegated to the home, they initiated a trend toward full participation in every area of the previously male-dominated society. Today, women are working next to men at the construction site, policing our neighborhoods, as well as fighting in partnership with men on the battlefield.

For the first time in history, women have control over their own bodies with breakthroughs in reproductive medicine which enable them to choose whether or not to have children. Women also have a choice in the number of children to have. There was no way a woman was going to work outside of the home while she had a dozen kids demanding her full time and attention. Some women may prefer to have many children, which is a perfectly valid choice, but at least it's a preference and not something forced upon her by circumstances.

Today, at the beginning of the 21st century, the progress achieved toward equality of the sexes would be substantially greater than it is if it hadn't been for the resistance of strong reactionary forces attempting to turn back the clock. Male-dominated organizations like higher education, politics, and religion vigorously tried to reassert their control over women but they were only successful in temporarily slowing down the inevitable surging tide of women's liberation.

Women are increasingly being voted into positions of power and, because of their new political authority, are ensuring continued progression toward full equality with men in every area of life.

If it weren't for women breaking free of their traditional roles, men would still be imprisoned by their own. Mankind is now at a point in our evolution where each gender is learning how to develop the positive qualities of the opposite gender.

Forty-year adjustment period

The initial women's movement of the 19th-century was the first forward charge in the battle against entrenched patriarchy. After the right for women to vote was established in all western countries, there was a general retreat of women's political action from approximately 1920 to 1960, at which time the current feminist movement got underway. This would be the final assault needed to shatter the rigidity of entrenched male-dominated culture worldwide. The influential women who took up the cause of equal pay for equal work and women's rights over their own bodies recaptured the high ground from the resistant male power structure of the undisputed equality of women and men in every area of life. The young seedlings of equality, which were planted by the resurgent women's movement of the

1960s, are now bearing fruit at the beginning of this 21st century.

It's not God or Goddess. It's God and Goddess

In order to shatter the illusion of male supremacy, the leaders of the feminist movement needed to tap into the deep reservoir of women's repressed rage and batter down the longstanding walls of male arrogance, ignorance and repression. In the process of doing so, some of these leaders attempted to elevate women to a place of superiority over men. For women to exchange roles with their captors by judging male energy as inferior would polarize the sexes and initiate a new cycle of war. In the process of judging males as inferior, various women leaders of the feminist movement got carried away and started expressing the very worst aspects of their own inner male energy by vigorously attacking and repressing all things male. They judged their inner feminine as being weak so they disconnected from compassion and over identified with anger. They tried to kill God off and replace him with the Goddess.

Fortunately, many of these same women are now realizing that in order to be whole as human beings we need a strong inner male as well as a strong inner female. They are reacquainting themselves with the positive aspects of their inner feminine qualities while honoring their inner male as well. Today, the women's movement is shifting to a holistic view that elevates the self-esteem of both women and men and this effort will bring victory to both. God and Goddess are two halves of the same Universal Creator. It's taken a long time but finally women and men are jointly assuming the thrones of power and will share equal authority in all areas of human endeavor.

We are now at a point in the collective consciousness of mankind where we no longer have to reaffirm the negative stereotypes of men and women. What we don't need is a reaffirmation of the past divisions between women and men by focusing on their differences. What we do require is a new vision of the dynamic possibilities awaiting us as both genders learn to accept and integrate the previously rejected male and female qualities within.

Women are from Earth... Men are from Earth

For so long men have expressed their male qualities of power, logic and strength while denying their female qualities of feeling, love and intuition. At the same time, women expressed their female qualities of feeling, love and intuition while suppressing their male qualities of power, logic and strength. At present, neither men nor women are complete personalities; each sex borrows its identity from a lack which the other supplies, and each requires the other for its completion. As women and men develop that completion out of themselves instead of looking to the other for it, they acquire true self reliance and independence, which is their common aspiration.

The challenge for women is to develop their male qualities of energy, logic, initiative, self control, generosity, courage, strength, assertiveness and leadership. These qualities point very clearly to the path of development which women must climb to achieve equality with men.

Men, on the other hand, if they don't want to be completely left behind by women, must develop their female qualities of feeling, intuition, love, patience, gentleness, forgiveness, refinement, nurturing, compassion, and sense of beauty.

New leadership: Power with Compassion

Leadership expressed without compassion is ruthless, while compassion expressed without power is impotent. For too long, the leaders in religion, government, arts and sciences were usually men who were totally out of touch with their inner female qualities and lacked warmth. The women who were standing right beside these men were out of tune with their inner male qualities and lacked power.

Today, as men and women become more balanced by embracing both their male and female qualities, a decidedly different type of leadership will fill the halls of power in every form of organization on the planet whether it is business, politics, religion or the arts and sciences.

Society will become gentler, more compassionate and more whole. The individuals who integrate their inner qualities of male and female will be put into positions of power all over the Earth and women will lead the way because, at this point in time, it's easier for a woman to accept and balance her masculine qualities than it is for a man to balance his feminine qualities.

Relationship roles transformed

The dynamics of intimate relationships have transformed because of human society's gradual acceptance of the complementary male and female qualities within. Women are no longer bound to the family and can express themselves through career while men are freed from the shackles of work and can choose to participate more in the home.

As men embrace their inner feminine qualities of nurturing and love, they are able to contribute more effectively to the nurturing of their children, giving women relief from the domestic responsibilities of the home. Women, tapping into their assertive male qualities, can now effectively stride forth into the marketplace, assisting men in bringing home more food.

Current Challenges for Men

Embrace your feelings: The primary challenge for men is to expand their ability to feel and express the full range of human emotions. Men have always had permission to feel and show anger but the vulnerable emotions such as sorrow, sympathy, and fear were strictly not allowed.

Men had no need to develop the feeling side of their nature because the women in their life would do the feeling for them. When a man is cut off from his feelings, it puts an unfair burden on the woman in his life because she winds up taking on his feelings in addition to her own. No wonder she may be a little over emotional at times! Additionally, because he is unfamiliar with the feeling realm, the woman in his life will often control him emotionally because that is her strength. Many a man has been a tiger in the boardroom, and a pussycat in the bedroom.

In order to be truly happy, men must unlock the doors of their hearts and allow their feelings to flow unrestricted. If a man's heart is filled with unexpressed sorrow, there is no room for him to experience the deeply joyful feelings of ecstasy and fulfillment. By learning to understand his feelings, he will be able to relate to the women in his life on an emotionally level playing field.

A man may accomplish remarkable goals but if his feelings are shut down, then there isn't any possibility of him experiencing a deep satisfaction in those successes. Man's inner feminine aspect of feeling allows him to slow down and fully savor his accomplishments. Otherwise he will move from achievement to achievement with no sense of emotional completion or contentment.

> *Men, open your heart willingly,*
> *or the universe will break your heart open.*
> Des Coroy.

If you look around, you'll notice that men all over the Earth are actually beginning to open their hearts, primarily because women all over the Earth are leaving them. It's through the crucible of pain that man is opening to his emotional nature.

Until recently, men didn't have to experience agonizingly painful feelings of abandonment because the women in their lives never left them. Now that women are embracing their ability to create economic independence for themselves, there's no reason for them to put up with an emotionally unresponsive man in their lives, so they leave.

For the first time in recorded history, men are faced with the hard-edged reality of being left alone with their grief. Often, they lose not only the woman in their lives but also their children.

It's through the ensuing process of deep grief that repressed feelings of fear, sorrow and anger come flooding through in an overwhelming waterfall of emotion. Men often feel as if their total life has come to an end, but all is not lost.

As a man progresses through his pain, he finally picks himself up and moves on. His experience of pain served as an emotional catalyst and he is a changed man. His heart was forced open by intense feelings of sorrow and fear and now he accepts and understands how to express previously unacknowledged emotions. In addition, he's probably learned to nurture himself by doing the physical things that he used to depend on his wife for, such as ironing, cooking, cleaning, and taking care of his children. Whether he wanted to or not, he's now in touch with the feminine part of his nature, his feelings.

Of course some men refuse to open their hearts even after the deep pain of divorce and quite often rush into the arms of a new woman who will again take on and process the man's disowned feelings. He then misses a big opportunity for growth.

There are easier ways of learning about your feelings than having to go through the devastation of abandonment. By voluntarily opening your heart to the gifts of your feelings, you will sidestep any painful lessons in your future.

Embrace the King within – There has been much confusion in the last 30 years around the shifting roles of men and women in society. Women demanded that men become more sensitive, which many of them did at the expense of suppressing some of their male qualities. Women had what they thought they wanted in a sensitive man who knew how to express his feelings but they were also turned off by this S.N.A.G. (sensitive new age guy) because the sexy part of him, his assertiveness, strength and charisma, were nowhere to be found. Everybody was confused. The men were confused because they worked on their feelings and eradicated the macho part of them and the women were still unhappy. The women were confused because they were mistaken in the assumption that if men became more sensitive and quit being so aggressive, they would be more than satisfied with their new man, and yet they weren't. Women discovered that they didn't want their men to become women. What they really wanted was for their boys to grow up and become men.

The old male model wouldn't do any more and the new model was too weak, so what was called for was a new vision of what it means to be male.

Men must keep their hearts open to their feeling nature while reassessing the dynamic qualities of their maleness. Men have to come to a place of maturity within themselves and learn to access the positive aspects of the king within them. The Inner King represents the constructive qualities of power, leadership, creativity, fatherhood, aspiration, productivity, logic, generosity, passion, support and strength. Men need these male qualities to balance the softer, feeling side of their nature. When men balance their strength with their compassion, women will naturally be attracted to them and feel safe at the same time. A man who is in touch with his positive Inner King has no need to dominate others because he shares power equally with his Queen.

Sharing domestic responsibilities – When men were the sole breadwinners of the family, they had no time whatsoever to participate in any domestic work around the home. Women, being home most the time, took care of the cooking, cleaning, buying food, and clothing the kids, along with the intensely focused responsibility of child-rearing. Many families maintain these traditional male and female roles with the man working out in the world and the woman working in the home, and for some couples it continues to be a perfectly valid choice.

Today, women are increasingly assuming the traditional

male role of working out in the world, often matching their male partner in time spent away from home. Women in the workforce have lightened the financial responsibility on men considerably with many women equaling or surpassing her man's take-home pay.

As women have lightened men's financial load, it's only fair that men lighten women's domestic load by physically assisting in the household responsibilities of cleaning, cooking, and caring for the children.

As a young man, I remember how resistant I was to doing any form of housework. I went from my family home of having my mother do everything for me, to an early marriage where my former wife took over the role of domestic servant from my mother. I didn't have to wash clothes, cook dinners, iron shirts, vacuum floors, clean windows, wash dishes, scrub toilets, change the kitty litter, change diapers, and night feed the baby. Nor did I have to be concerned about the children's schooling, health, homework, feeding, transportation and emotional nurturing. My wife took care of everything, so all I had to do was go to work, enjoy a few beers with my friends on the way home, and eat a delicious meal which was always waiting for me on the table.

When my wife started to work full-time, she requested that I participate more in the responsibilities of the home. I told her I was much too busy at the office to get involved with any housework and that she would have to deal with it. It wasn't long before my wife started having migraines every time I wanted to have sex. I also noticed mysterious scorch marks on my white shirts, sand in my beer, consistently bitter coffee and smaller portions of food on my plate. I think she was trying to get my attention but I just continued to ignore her pleas for assistance around the house.

It wasn't until after we separated and finally divorced that I realized I hadn't been carrying my weight around the home. It wasn't the only reason we parted ways but it certainly didn't help matters. Living alone for the first time in my life, I experienced a crash course on how to do housework, cook, and fully care for my daughters every second weekend.

Women are experiencing incredible stress trying to

balance work, children and the duties of the home. If men would do their fair share around the home, it would greatly reduce women's stress levels in all areas.

It's particularly important for a man to help out with childcare when a new child is born into the family. The first three months is especially taxing to a woman's health because of erratic sleep patterns and physical exhaustion. If a man would be willing to alternate getting up for the child's feeding, that alone would make a huge difference to the woman's ability to recuperate from the long pregnancy and birth. Besides helping reduce his wife's burdens, he also develops his nurturing abilities to a fuller degree.

Fair is fair. As men, we can't expect women to work full-time without us equally pitching in and sharing the responsibilities of home and family. Sometimes men will use the excuse of having to put in a lot of hours at work in order to avoid the responsibilities at home. If you say that you don't have the time and you're making good money, please consider hiring someone to come in every couple of weeks and give the house a thorough cleaning, or hire a nanny part-time. You might as well get with the program because women are no longer putting up with our laziness. Appealing to your logic, it's far better to do 50 percent of the housework now than to do 100 percent of it after she leaves you.

It doesn't always have to be 50-50 because your circumstances will be unique to you. Maybe your partner is working part time and you are putting in a lot of hours at work, then of course you may only do 30 percent of the housework. On the other hand, you may be working part time or be between jobs and you may contribute 80 percent of the effort around the home and family while your partner works full time in her career. The only rule is to be fair with each other and come to an agreement which satisfies both of you. Your partner will appreciate your efforts around the home and you will immediately notice a positive change in your relationship because you won't have a physically and emotionally exhausted woman in the house devising ways to poison your food.

Current challenges for Women

Embrace your assertiveness – One of the primary challenges for women today is to learn how to access their inner male qualities of assertiveness and power. For far too long women have had to hide their power from others. It was considered unladylike for a woman to directly put forth her point of view. Women who were assertive were mistakenly considered to be aggressive. Often words like "bitch" were hurled at them as a way to humiliate them back into their place. There was considerable social pressure placed on women to hide their authority and power so as not to appear too aggressive. It's not that women didn't wield power. In many ways their power actually surpassed the men in their life because it was a covert and hidden influence that worked very effectively behind the scenes. Their control wasn't apparent on the surface because women used the skills of manipulation to get what they wanted in life. They had to maneuver people and situations in a non-direct way because directly asking for what they wanted was considered too forceful.

It's important to distinguish between the two words aggressive and assertive. Aggressive means combative, quarrelsome, attacking and belligerent. Assertive means self-confident, firm, bold, emphatic and definite. Assertiveness is a positive quality that empowers a woman to directly ask for what she wants in life. Rather than hide her power in a thicket of ulterior motives, she can choose to assertively put forth her views and requirements in an above-board, direct and to-the-point manner.

Women can save themselves lots of time and energy by being assertively direct with others because manipulation is a twisting route which requires plenty of effort. Another reason to move away from the manipulative path to power is because it is rooted in deception. Deception of all kinds erodes our self-esteem. (By the way, men can be just as skilled in the art of manipulation.) At one time it was necessary for women to manipulate situations because they were dominated by men but here at the beginning of the 21st century, as women embrace their inner male authority in the world, the assertive path to power will bring women much greater rewards.

Balancing home and career – Finding the proper balance between time spent in the home and time dedicated to career is one of the biggest challenges facing women today. In the last 50 years, women have moved into the workforce in astounding numbers. From airline pilots to police officers, from physicians to politicians, from scientists to astronauts, women have penetrated every previously male-dominated profession and have produced amazing results. These women were leaders of their time who set a target for the masses of women to follow. Women still have a way to go before they equally share power with men in politics, religion, business and science. As of this writing, a wage gap still exists, with women in most western countries only making 77 percent of men's earnings in the same job.

Many women today are proactive in their careers and have established financial independence for themselves. Because of the financial pressures in today's world, it's sometimes very difficult for a family to get by on just the husband's income and women are often forced to work. In fact, quite a large percentage of women spend too many hours away from the home and have a tendency to overwork. Finding a balance between the two is important to women's emotional and physical well-being as well as to the health of their children.

Mother envy

There has been much written about mothers by the previous generation who surrendered their careers for the sake of being at home full-time with their children. It has been stated that their daughters had more freedom of choice in career and chose to exercise that freedom by becoming successful in the business world. Often these mothers were both supportive of their daughters' careers and jealous at the same time. They rejoiced in their daughters' successes while often feeling regret for not developing and expressing their own creative and business skills. What has not been discussed at any length is that many of the daughters who chose career over family have secretly and quite often unconsciously been jealous of their mother not having to work at all. If they're honest with themselves, many of today's superwomen who juggle work and home have a part of them that would love to be totally supported financially by the man in their life and be able to stay home with the children. Many of these career-oriented daughters are finally admitting that being able to spend more time with their children would bring more joy into their lives.

Women are discovering the fact that it doesn't have to be all business or all family but it can be a blend of both. Career-oriented women have an opportunity to allow themselves the time to spend more time with their children by choosing to spend a little less time in work, just as family-oriented women have an opportunity to allow themselves the time to spend more time at work by choosing to spend a little less time in the family.

Traditionally there has been a polarization between women who worked and the ones who stayed at home with children. Today at the beginning of the 21st century, the dividing line between stay-at-home mothers and working women is not nearly as defined as some would like you to believe. There is much more fluidity in women's choices, with some women choosing to flow in and out of the work arena. A woman may work for a few years and then choose to stay home for a time and then at a later date choose to work again.

Many factors are converging to allow women more choice in the challenge of balancing the responsibilities of her family and career. Men's growing participation in assuming the tasks of family and home is liberating more time for women to expand outward in their careers.

Dynamic changes in the corporate climate have produced a new mix of employment options for women such as flextime, outsourcing, and parental leave. Telecommuting or telework give women the opportunity to work from home using modern means of communication such as the Internet. Female entrepreneurs are also developing home-based small businesses which present them with the opportunity to stay close to the children while providing a source of income and accomplishment.

Even with the expanded variety of choices in a woman's career options, finding a balance between home and work will remain a difficult challenge for some years to come. Single mothers have an especially difficult time achieving harmony between family and career while still creating time for their own personal needs. As women enter the decision-making arena of politics, new laws will be passed to support women in their quest for relief from the enormous pressure of finding an equilibrium between work and family responsibilities. With women's ascension into corporate leadership positions worldwide, we will see a dramatically increased empathetic response to women's needs within the work environment.

Create your own financial resources: Numerous women are still unemployed and it's to these women that the following words are addressed. In order to be totally free within a relationship with a man, a woman needs to also create her own financial resources if possible.

Why is it so important that women achieve personal economic independence? Until recently, women had no personal financial wealth to fall back upon in times of need. Women depended on the men in their lives to provide financial security. The deal that was struck between men and women was, "I'll take care of your emotional needs, my husband, if you take care of my financial needs."

The deal worked fine until there was some type of angry disruption in the relationship. As a method of control, each sex had a weapon to wield. The woman controlled her man by cutting off the flow of love while the man controlled his woman by cutting off the flow of funds.

How to marry a millionaire and be enslaved at the same time

In the past, when women were not able to generate money for themselves, they often depended on finding a man who had some. Today women have unlimited opportunity to financially create their own wealth and no longer need to depend on a man for it. However, some women are reluctant to forsake the dream of marrying somebody with wealth.

Even if a woman connects with a partner who is financially wealthy, if she chooses to be totally dependent on him financially, often it comes at a great price. The cost to her will be her independence because men of wealth are accustomed to owning things. He will pay for everything she desires with his money and she will pay for everything she receives with her freedom.

A woman often has trouble exercising freedom of choice within her relationship because her husband is responsible for her financial sustenance. Often a man attempts to prevent his partner from working because he unconsciously fears her newfound freedoms of choice.

If a woman wanted to divorce, often she wasn't able to do so for financial reasons, so she endured. She was stuck in a loveless marriage simply because she didn't have the financial security she needed to leave. Even if she were able to leave the marriage, it's an established fact that after divorce, women, along with their children, are usually the major losers in the ability to maintain their quality of life, contrary to what many believe.

Another reason a woman may give for not being able to work is that she may choose to stay home with the kids so that she can give them her full attention and nurturing. Working in some sort of career seems out of the question. If she is employed outside of the home, even if it's only part-time, she may feel that her children will suffer because of it.

Many women become emotionally enmeshed with their children to the point that their primary interest is the children and the children only. Sometimes women will unconsciously look to their children to fill the emotional gap that is missing from the relationship with their male partner. This emotional weight creates enormous pressure on the children which they are not capable of handling. There is a fine line between effective mothering and oppressive smothering.

A woman having outside interests, such as a career or educational pursuits, will greatly enrich her life, expand her world and take the burden off her children to fill her emotional well. If a woman lives only through her children she'll bypass opportunities to stimulate her mind by expressing herself in imaginatively productive ways. She will also deprive herself of economic independence and the ability to financially contribute to her husband's efforts at creating monetary security for the family.

Is it possible for a woman to successfully nurture her children and still be able to follow the dreams which will expand her way of life? I believe she can.

If the man in her life starts helping at home with the domestic responsibilities and caring for the children, her time will be freed to pursue outside interests which utilize her intellect. As men become more nurturing and value quality time with their family, women will benefit immensely by not being restricted to the home. A woman challenged by study or work is a woman tapping into deep inner resources of intelligence, creativity and passion.

> The great renewal of the world will perhaps consist in this, that man and maid, freed of all false feelings and reluctances, will seek each other not as opposites, but as brother and sister, as neighbors, and will come together as human beings.
> Rainer Maria Rilke, (1875 - 1926),
> German poet.

It will take time to move into equilibrium between men and women and you can be certain that we will fall down along the way. After all, it takes time to learn how to ride a bike. But as sure as the world turns and the Earth moves around the sun, the day will come within the next few generations when men and women will experience themselves to be two halves of the same human species, co-equal partners in this game called life.

Chapter 13

Outside Interference

The marvelous richness of human experience would lose something of rewarding joy if there were no limitations to overcome. The hilltop hour would not be half so wonderful if there were no dark valleys to traverse.
Helen Keller, (1880 – 1968),
American blind/deaf author, lecturer, amorist.

Up to now we have focused on the internal influences which can affect your relationship. Now we will explore some of the external influences which can disrupt your partnership.

There are three major outside interferences which can cause serious damage to your partnership:
- **Children**
- **Family and friends**
- **Stress**

Children = Sextinguishers

Kids possess an uncanny knack for putting out the fires of your passion. It's difficult to shift from lying down next to your child while reading them a bedtime story to walking into the next room and lying down next to your partner with a totally different goal in mind.

Remember when you and your partner made hot, passionate love on the dining room table? (If you haven't, give it a try, as it's highly recommended.) Now the only time you make love on the table is when you and your child sit there drawing pink hearts for Valentine's Day. Children can cause enormous stress on the romantic bonds of your relationship. When you and your partner first dated your whole world revolved around each other. Sex was spontaneous, romance was alive and time was a commodity you freely shared with each other. After children arrive, often everything changes. Sex is planned, romance is dead and no one has time for anything.

It's just a fact of life that dependent children will require an enormous amount of your time and effort but there are a few simple things you can do to redirect some of the energy spent on the children back into your relationship.

a) Make your bedroom sacred and private – When the children are able to come in and out of your bedroom whenever they choose, it destroys any sense of privacy for you and your partner. While having sex, if you're worried about the door opening at any moment and one of your children walking in just as you're reaching the big 'O', there's no way that either of you will be totally present in your climactic experience.

Privacy is not something that I'm merely entitled to, it's an absolute prerequisite.
Marlon Brando, (1924 –),
American actor, director.

Create sanctuary for yourself and your partner by putting a lock on the door and telling the children to knock if the door is closed. It's always better to deal with a small child who's crying because they can't get into your bedroom than for you to be crying because your five-year-old just discovered wild animals on your bed.

b) Use babysitters often – Parents with young children are often afraid to leave their children with a babysitter or even a relative. They are under the illusion that their child will suffer irreparable damage if the parents choose to go out on the town for a night. For many parents, even dinner and a movie is out of the question.

By refusing to go out on dates with your partner because of your unfounded fear of "abandoning" your child, you automatically devalue the importance of keeping a strong romantic connection between each other. At the very least, plan weekly dates with each other, utilizing the services of a family member or professional babysitter to care for your children. Financial considerations shouldn't matter because even if things are a bit tight, you can still plan outings that cost little or no money.

The most important thing is that you and your partner have valuable alone time together on a regular basis. Believe me, the children also need a break from you. You're also teaching them by your example a valuable lesson on how to nurture their future relationship by balancing the responsibilities of raising children with the responsibilities of keeping romance alive.

c) Create compromise and agreement on child rearing – No issue creates more disharmony in a relationship than for partners to have opposing viewpoints on how to raise their children. Coming from different childhood experiences yourselves, it's natural that you sometimes possess different views on the best way to set limits for your children.

> *A torn jacket is soon mended; but hard words bruise the heart of a child.*
> Henry Wadsworth Longfellow, (1819 – 1892), American poet.

If one of you feels that the other is being too harsh or too lenient in the disciplinary process with your children, resentments can build to a point where they will disrupt your relationship.

With the increase in blended families, it makes it even more difficult because both children and parents have to adjust to totally different ways of child rearing. Whatever family dynamic you find yourself in, it's important for both partners to come to a clear understanding of your individual approaches to raising children. Ideally it's best to come to an agreement before the children arrive on the scene but you can create an accord at any time. Compromise and negotiation are the necessary tools you will need to establish an important middle ground between your viewpoints. I have found the Talking Stick to be an effective guide to navigating the turbulent waters of parental negotiations.

Children are masters at exploiting any differences between you and your partner in order to get what they want. They do this by playing you against each other so it's vital that you always show a strong consensus in front of your children, even if you disagree with the way your partner has handled things. No matter how angry you are, wait until both of you have a private moment when you can discuss your differences and arrive at an agreed-upon compromise which will work for the two of you.

I remember my father being especially strict with me at times in my childhood. All I had to do was run to my mother, who I had wrapped around my little finger, squeeze out a few crocodile tears about my feelings being hurt, and she would often go behind his back and give me what I wanted, saying, "Don't tell your father. It's our little secret." Secretly supporting your child's wishes by aligning with them against your partner totally undermines the united parental authority that you both have established.

> When I was a kid my parents moved a lot, but I always found them.
>
> Rodney Dangerfield,
> American comedian, actor.

Remember, unless your partner is abusing the children emotionally or physically, try not to interfere by disagreeing in front of the children. Supporting each other in the process of raising your children will make it much easier for both of you because your children will be less inclined to manipulate you against each other to get what they want.

Family and friends

Family members and well-meaning friends have been the source of many an argument within an intimate relationship. Parents are especially challenged in trying to stay out of their adult children's affairs. Many parents have a tendency to interfere in their children's relationships in a variety of ways. From choice of partner to choice of marriage venue, from choice of residence to choice in the number of grandchildren, parents can be way too absorbed in their children's lives.

Because most parents have 20 to 30 years more experience than their children, they feel as if they will always be wiser, smarter and more experienced than their children. However, having more experience does not necessarily equate to having more intelligence or wisdom. In fact once a child reaches the age of 30 in today's fast world, the experience level is probably equal to 45 years of their parents' generation. Sometimes parents may see things more clearly in a situation but that doesn't give them an automatic right to make pronouncements on how their children should live.

As a father of three intelligent young women, I had to learn to stay out of my children's relationships unless I was invited to give my point of view. Sometimes I didn't agree with their choice in partner and could see that they were probably headed for heartache. I had to bite my tongue to prevent me from speaking my mind. A few times my daughters did experience emotional pain through a relationship choice that went astray but it was a lesson that they had to go through. Short of an abusive situation, I won't interfere in their relationships. I may share my concerns with them but then it's important for me to let go of the situation.

Let your children go if you want to keep them.
Malcolm S. Forbes, (1919 – 1990),
American publisher, businessman.

With the increase in world immigration, the last 30 years

have seen a large influx of immigrants from Europe, South America and Asia, with strong conservative family values. The children of these immigrants often develop more progressive choices in their lifestyle that conflict with their parents' wishes. I have often seen the pain that results from parents demanding that their children culturally live a certain way. Some parents put tremendous pressure on their children to reject the partner that they choose because he or she doesn't meet their approval for social or religious reasons.

If you're a parent who has a tendency to interfere in your children's lives, please allow them the space and freedom to make their own choices, even if it's in opposition to what you may choose. Many of you are concerned about your children and feel that it is your right as responsible parents to tell them what to do. In actuality, you have no rights over your children at all. You can make suggestions but not commands. Remember, your children are a gift to you from the Creator and they are not your property. If your children ask for your opinion, by all means offer it once and then allow them the space to choose their own path in life. After all, you wouldn't put up with anyone telling you how to live your life, so why should you attempt to control your children's lives? It certainly didn't feel good when your parents attempted to dominate your life. Now you have an opportunity to break the chain of control tactics which has been passed down from generation to generation and to allow your children freedom of choice.

Interference in your relationship is not limited to parents, because brothers, sisters, cousins, aunts, uncles, children and friends are equally capable of causing damage.

Here are a few key tips which may help to protect your relationship from unwanted interference.

a) Keep your relationship private – When difficulties arise in our relationships, we have a tendency to want to openly share our problems with people close to us such as family and friends. Often we will find emotional support from someone outside of our relationship because we are much too angry or hurt to get support from our partner. It feels good at the time to receive sympathy, especially if the person sides with us and agrees that we have been wronged by our partner. In addition, you may receive erroneous advice from them which can make your situation worse.

The problem arises when you spill the dirt on your partner in great detail to someone who will then know way too much about an issue that should have remained an extremely private matter between you and your partner. Because your friend or family member is protective of you, they will no longer view your partner in the same positive way as before you gave them the inside scoop. For example, if one of my daughters called me up crying on the phone telling me that she suspects that her husband is having an affair, how do you think I'm going to feel about him? Even if she discovers that she was mistaken, will I ever look at him in quite the same way?

What if your best friend informs you that his wife has a drinking problem and that he is constantly abused by her? No matter how hard you try you won't be able to perceive her in the same way. Even if she sobers up and stops the abuse your outlook of her will be forever altered by her husband's breach of privacy.

> What is told into the ear of a man is often heard a hundred miles away.
>
> Chinese proverb.

Unless you are in a physically or emotionally desperate situation, keep your relationship issues private by keeping your family and friends out of it. If you need to talk to someone about your concerns or problems, find a professional counselor and pay for their time.

Everyone is faced with difficult issues in their intimate relationship, but sharing the private intimacies of your union with others violates the sacred trust which exists between you and your partner. People can give you sympathy, advice and points of view, but ultimately the only way to work through problems in your relationship is by your mutual courage to communicate clearly, fairly and with a high degree of personal integrity.

b) Don't triangulate – To triangulate is when two individuals team up against a third person in order to win. For example, let's say that you feel that your partner should not be attending night school because it takes her away from your kids, yet she refuses to compromise on her schooling because it's important to her. You call her mother and have a discussion about your concerns and she agrees with you that her daughter should stay at home with the children. The next time you and your partner have a discussion about her leaving school you say, "Well it's not only me that thinks you're being irresponsible to the kids, but I've talked to your mother about it and she agrees that it's in the children's best interest that you quit immediately." Sound familiar?

We triangulate in order to put pressure on another person to get them to do what we want. It's an unfair tactic that's a form of gossip which can involve family and friends in your personal disagreements and cause them to choose sides. Often you will never know that someone has triangulated against you because it was done secretly, behind your back, with the intention of changing an opinion about you. It's fairly common in most families to triangulate at one time or another but to continue doing it yourself is poisonous to your relationship.

Rest satisfied with doing well, and leave others to talk of you as they will.
Pythagoras, (BC 582 – 507), Greek philosopher, mathematician.

If someone approaches you with the intention of enlisting your support against a third person, it's important that you resist the urge to triangulate. It can be difficult to resist because we all have an inquisitive part of us which likes to hear gossip about others. However, the information you hear about someone else may be totally inaccurate and your opinion of this other person may be negatively affected.

Triangulation is a manipulation and the reason it works is that we are often too concerned about what others think about us.

When someone starts to triangulate by using gossip, gently steer away from the topic. If the person persists by bringing it up again, it's very important to let them know that you are not interested in talking about someone else while they are not there to defend themselves. As a last resort, you can always walk away. By doing so you break the other person's ability to triangulate with you and you remain loyal to your partner or friend.

> Great minds discuss ideas;
> average minds discuss events;
> small minds discuss people.
> — Source unknown.

The next time someone tries to triangulate with someone else by teaming up against you, politely inform them that you are absolutely not interested in what someone else has to say and that you are only interested in hearing their own opinion. If someone says to you that the whole world feels you're doing the wrong thing, tell them that you could not care less about anyone else's point of view and that you'll only discuss their own. Be consistent and you will put a stop to the manipulation once and for all.

c) Troublesome friends or acquaintances – Unfortunately, sometimes the people we consider to be friends are not safe to be around because they may be toxic to the health of your relationship. It's important as a couple for you to identify the people who are supportive of your relationship. Occasionally, friendships that were established before your current relationship can cause problems. A long-known friend from your past might have difficulty adjusting to spending less time with you and could unconsciously get possessive. Petty jealousies and competitiveness from some individuals can interfere in your relationship if you allow it.

Trust your feelings and if you both continue to feel uncomfortable with a friend then it's important to discuss the situation with the friend in order to sort things out, but ultimately you must stand with your partner.

> May God defend me from my friends; I can defend myself from my enemies.
>
> Voltaire, (1694 – 1778),
> French historian, writer.

Perhaps you are close friends with someone and your partner does not feel safe with your friend. You and your partner may have totally different perceptions of the other person's intentions. It's very important to allow your partner's opposing view to be expressed. As long as this is not a situation where one of you is being jealous of the other's friend, it's essential to take the time to communicate with each other about the perceived danger.

There is usually a valid reason for your partner's perception because sometimes we have blind spots to what's going on around us. Always give your partner the benefit of the doubt.

Choose your friends wisely and always trust your intuition because there are too many trustworthy people in the world to have to tolerate anything less.

Stress

We now live in an extremely fast-paced world culture. Compared to the 19th century, there has been a dramatic increase in the level of stress that the average human being experiences on a daily basis. We are bombarded with an amazing variety of stress-inducing agents which tax our physical, emotional and mental wellbeing to the limit.

In large cities, many people commute to and from work by car, sometimes driving an hour or more in each direction. Driving in heavy traffic and attempting to avoid danger on the road produces high levels of daily stress.

We are exposed to thousands of toxic chemicals in our air,

water, and even our food supply, which greatly stresses our physical body. From microwaves to radio waves, from x-rays to household magnetic fields, from television towers to cellular phones, our human cells slowly simmer in an amazing stew of invisible electromagnetic energy. Television and newspaper media assault our minds daily with negative images of destructive events occurring worldwide.

No wonder you may be a little stressed out by the time you get home! When you add the burden of balancing the responsibilities of career and family, you can fully understand that the cumulative stresses of modern life put enormous pressure on human relationships. Stress is very insidious in that we are often unaware of just how wound up we really are at any given time.

When you and your partner see each other at the end of a busy day, you're often like two coiled serpents ready to strike. It doesn't take much to spark an argument that could release the pent-up stress all at once. Stress causes us to overreact with our partners, our children, and the family pet. It happens all the time.

Many stressful situations such as war, disease, natural disasters, and in-laws are beyond your direct control. However, you do have authority over two main factors which often negatively affect your relationship — **financial stress and physical/ emotional stress.**

Money pressures can cause a tremendous strain on any relationship. Lack of sufficient funds comes in right behind children as a major cause of stress within a relationship. Most couples are totally unprepared for the financial pressures which they will encounter in life. Unfortunately most of us have not been properly trained in the art of managing money. We just learn along the way. Many of the lessons about money are exceedingly painful ones which can shake the foundation of any relationship.

Money in our culture represents security, freedom and the power to provide for the needs of the relationship. When money is in short supply, all of these areas will suffer and the union between you and your partner will be strained.

> Love without money is just as barren as money without love.
>
> Des Coroy.

If Romeo and Juliet hadn't had to depend on their family's money and had some of their own, they could have left Italy on the next boat for France and we may have had a totally different end to their story.

Money problems magnify all other problems in life. The little stresses and strains of daily life become exaggerated and blown out of proportion when we are financially insecure. Many more relationships crumble under the weight of financial burden than are destroyed by sexual affairs.

Live within your means

We live in a materialistic world that ruthlessly promotes consumerism as the path to fulfillment in life. From a young age we are fed a steady diet of television and print advertising conditioning us to always seek new and improved, more, better and the latest in consumer merchandise.

Being mentally programmed to purchase, a typical young couple often find themselves buying products which are far beyond their purchasing power. If they're not careful, continued purchase after purchase will put them into heavy debt and place them on the road to financial ruin. Relationships are tough enough without adding the additional burden of economic devastation.

Quite often, jointly working through financial difficulties can be very strengthening to a relationship. However, if you can avoid money misery, the road to abundance can be just as strengthening and a lot more fun.

> I'm not into the money thing.
> You can only sleep in one bed at a time.
> You can only eat one meal at a time, or be in one car at a time. So I don't have to have millions of dollars to be happy. All I need are clothes on my back, a decent meal, and a little loving when I feel like it.
> That's the bottom line.
>
> Ray Charles, (1930 -),
> American musician, singer, songwriter.

Start looking at ways of avoiding money difficulties by resisting the knee-jerk reaction of purchasing products that you don't really need. For example, a new car purchase can be one of the worst "investments" you can make because it has a terrible value depreciation over the first few years. Who says you have to purchase a new car every three or four years? Anyway, you only enjoy that new car smell for about two months before reality sets in and you lose interest in its newness because the monthly car payment is due. If you provide a car with proper maintenance, it will last a lot longer than four years. By holding onto your car, you will at least get lots more value out of it and you won't be making perpetual car payments.

There are many other impulse purchases we make that waste our money. Do you really need that amazing new digital camera which massages your shoulders as you snap a photo, while an audio recording continues to repeat how beautiful you looked in that last picture? Perhaps not.

By all means, if you have the money, you're financially liquid, and you have the freedom to purchase what you want without going into debt, enjoy yourself and buy to your heart's content. On the other hand, if you're struggling to make ends meet and you're not sure how you are going to pay next month's bills, then consider rejecting any purchase that you can live without so that you will not put unneeded financial pressure on your and your partner's life.

Simplicity
Simpli/city
Live Simply in the City

Our world is incredibly complex, with an amazing number of possible lifestyle choices for us to make. In considering those choices, we often get caught up in the buzz of material living, thinking that if we buy enough and own enough, we will somehow be happy. We often forget that the simplest choice can be the most fulfilling. Maybe it's not the things of life that your soul is desiring but it's the essence of life that you are seeking. Value choices of knowledge, love, exploration and community may have a much better chance of filling your well.

Here are a few tips that may help reduce financial pressures:

1) Use credit cards only when absolutely necessary

Personal credit card debt is now at an all-time high. Many individuals have three or more credit cards continually maxed to the limit and are paying incredibly high interest rates for the pleasure of doing so.

Some financial institutions even have point schemes to encourage you to use your card where you have to charge $15,000 on it so you can claim a $50 airline ticket discount. Get your credit card debt down to zero as quickly as you can and keep it there. Use your card for necessary purchases and strive to pay it off by the end of the month.

For many of you who have become addicted to using a credit card, it will mean some considerable changes to your lifestyle in order to achieve zero balance. Credit card use can be an addiction that is harder to shake than cigarettes. It will take time to kick your credit card habit, so be patient and chip away at it. The joy you'll experience when you see that zero balance on your monthly invoice will be well worth the effort.

> If your outgo exceeds your income, then your upkeep will be your downfall.
> Bill Earle.

2) Plan a budget that you can keep

For most people, planning budgets certainly wouldn't be considered fun. It lies somewhere between paying taxes and visiting your dentist, yet if you don't have a budget, chances are you are wasting a sizable amount of your financial resources. There is an old saying that, "A small hole can sink a big ship." You work so hard for your money. Why would you allow it to leak through your hands because of impulsive spending?

Sit down with your partner and plan a budget which allows flexibility so that you both won't feel too restricted. You're much more likely to keep within your budgetary limits if you allow for some spontaneous spending.

You may have different ideas that will need to be clearly communicated and the Talking Stick would be a great tool for you to negotiate compromises. After agreeing on a budget, the mutual self-discipline required to adhere to it will provide you with a sense of accomplishment and increased self-esteem, and the extra money saved can be applied to paying off debt or used to create investments.

> Modern man is frantically trying to earn enough to buy things he's too busy to enjoy.
> Frank A. Clark.

3) Eliminate debt, save money and invest it

Long-term debt such as a mortgage gives most individuals the only possible way to afford a home. Paying it off prior to the term of the loan will save you a small fortune. Resist the temptation to borrow against the equity in your home by taking out a second mortgage for such luxury items as that boat you've always wanted, or funding your European cruise.

Borrow against your home only in the event of an emergency or for using the capital as the seed money in another sound investment.

Financial debt keeps you in economic slavery

Live within your income. Resist the temptation to buy a $30,000 car when you can only afford a $15,000 car. Don't over-extend yourself for the sake of a temporary buying impulse. It isn't worth it to put pressure on yourself for the sake of owning something that you really don't need, even if everybody in your neighborhood owns one. Today, personal and family debt is at an all-time high in most Western nations. Excessively buying things on credit restricts your life by keeping you in financial bondage.

As you reduce your overall debt, you will free up money for investment purposes. A good way to get into the habit of saving money is to take 10 percent of your wage and pay yourself by putting it into a savings account that is totally separate from your checking account.

After working hard for your money, the least you can do is keep 10 percent of what you make. If, for some reason, the thought of giving yourself 10 percent of your earnings makes you feel guilty, remember that you probably pay over 30 percent in income tax and an additional 10 percent of your income in sales taxes. When your pay is deposited in the bank, pay yourself first by withdrawing 10 percent of it immediately and placing it into a separate account. You deserve it.

After you have accumulated savings, it's time to seek ways of investing it. Real estate, stock, or investing in yourself by using it for education or a small business are a few ways you might apply it. It's important to take full financial responsibility for yourself and your family because no government is coming to the rescue.

The financial opportunities for growing money have never been better.

Money isn't everything but if you don't have a sustainable amount of it, life in our society can be miserable and your relationship will slowly wilt from the lack of it.

> If you know how to spend less than you get, you have the philosopher's stone.
> Benjamin Franklin, (1706 – 1790),
> American scientist, publisher, diplomat.

4) Seek a financial adviser if needed

A good financial adviser not only can assist you in investing your money in the best possible location, but he or she can also support you in eradicating debt. Some men and women are very sensitive about disclosing their lack of financial knowledge to another person, so they may resist seeking support.

When we have a physical illness, we don't hesitate to go to a professional physician for guidance in healing. Likewise, when faced with a financial illness, there should be no shame attached to utilizing the professional skills of a financial adviser to help you heal your money problems.

5) Physical, mental, and emotional stress

All three are intertwined in one way or another. If you are physically stressed and tired, it will affect your mood. If you're under mental pressure at work, your physical vitality could be reduced. Environmental stress, work-related stress, the stress of children and emotional stress all have a major impact on the quality of your relationship. If you are overwhelmed in any of these areas your relationship will suffer. It's hard to be warm and loving to your partner when you're getting ready to explode from internal pressures.

One of the greatest antidotes to stress of all kinds is to strengthen your physical health by exercising regularly, balancing nutritional intake. and reducing exposure to environmental toxins. Drugs of all kinds, whether prescriptive or recreational, cigarettes, excessive alcohol, and unnecessary contact with poisonous chemicals in your surroundings all work aggressively against achieving maximum physical health. If you're not physically healthy, achieving mental and emotional health is much more difficult.

When you're physically strong and vibrant, you're in a much better position to handle the daily stresses and strains which impinge upon you and your relationship. Issues that arise between you and your new partner tend to be worked through without needless drama. You tend to not let things get to you as much when you are vitally alive.

When you're physically exhausted and unwell, it's easy for the smallest issues to get blown way out of proportion within your relationship. Allowing your body to run down negatively affects your mental and emotional well-being.

The natural state of a human being is radiant health. Today, what we accept as the norm is certainly a good deal below that level. The average person is sleep deprived, nutritionally weak and physically out of shape.

It's inevitable that health levels will decline along with mental and emotional attitudes as long as you refuse to put the time and effort into taking full responsibility for your personal physical health.

Life demands purity in water, food, and air

It takes work to get healthy, as well as a strong commitment to making it happen. You have to start paying attention to what you eat. Simple dietary changes which replace lifeless denatured grains and sugar with life affirming whole grains and honey or stevia can make a huge difference to your energy levels. Drinking purified water, minus the unnecessary poisons of chlorine and fluoride which flow from your kitchen tap, could go a long way toward establishing better health. You have to exercise regularly and not just talk about doing it. Besides strengthening your muscles and internal organs, exercise helps you release pent-up stresses, such as anger and mental anxiety, in a positive way.

Get out of the ant hill

In a relationship, the stresses of work and family allow little time for individual personal alone time. It's very important to have individual private time away from your partner and children. Many of you may be thinking at this point, "There is no way I would have any time for myself as I am much too busy with my responsibilities." If you feel this way, then please consider altering your viewpoint to allow time for yourself to recharge your physical, mental, and emotional batteries. It doesn't have to be a lot of time. Fifteen minutes a day in your garden may be all that you need to effectively let go of accumulated stress. Maybe it's just a daily half-hour walk which will soothe your soul. Perhaps allowing yourself the time to meditate or write in a journal would be your key to relaxing. One of my favorite ways of releasing stress is to receive a therapeutic massage on a regular basis. Whatever way you choose, allowing yourself the necessary time to be alone in the world without anyone making physical, mental, or emotional demands on you is vital to your total health and well-being.

> *For fast-acting relief try slowing down.*
> Lily Tomlin, (1939 -),
> American comedienne.

With strong physical health you're less likely to be negatively affected by the mental and emotional stresses of daily life. Still, many people are experiencing deep levels of emotional depression, which have a strong impact on their relationships. If a person is depressed, all perceptions about their relationship will be filtered through their depressive state, and joy in the relationship will fly right out the window. Depression is not only difficult for the person experiencing it but it is also a major challenge to the partner who isn't depressed. It's very common for one person to be depressed while the other partner is also depressed but isn't aware of it or is in denial. If the partner who is experiencing depression seeks professional counseling, then it would be very supportive for the other partner to also participate in the counseling sessions. At the very least the supportive partner would learn coping skills for how to deal more effectively with their partner's depression.

There are many factors contributing to the causes of depression. The roots of depression are often deep and complex. Overwork can physically and emotionally exhaust an individual to the point where depression sets in. With global corporate downsizing and realignment, unexpected and undesired career changes which threaten financial security can precipitate a period of depression. Many men's feelings of self worth are attached to their career and when they lose their job, depression often is the result.

> It's a recession when your neighbor loses his job;
> it's a depression when you lose your own.
> Harry S. Truman, (1884-1972),
> Thirty-third President of the USA.

Depression is often triggered by nutritional deficiencies or hormonal fluctuations in both men and women. Endocrine gland imbalances such as from the thyroid can be a cause. An alarming percentage of women are experiencing early menopause and infertility in their mid to late 30s. (There is alarming scientific evidence of an increase in estrogen levels in our food supply and environment which could be causative factors in the worldwide epidemic of infertility, early puberty and menopause.) This can be particularly devastating to these young women because they experience a double whammy of massive hormonal fluctuations but also an unexpected grieving process over children they are no longer able to bear. Deep depression is often a result.

With many individuals, repressed anger is at the root of their depression because the life force required to contain anger emotionally drains them. Vigorous regular exercise can often get blocked energies moving again and free stagnant emotions which may have been feeding the depression.

Besides traditional medicine's approach of using

antidepressants, there is a growing body of alternative medical treatments which are very effective against many forms of depression. In Europe, antidotes to depression such as the medicinal herb St. John's Wort and SAM-e, have been prescribed as extensively as chemical antidepressants. Either choice should be supplemented with extensive therapeutic counseling to get to the causes of depression. Otherwise, drug or alternative therapies will just mask the symptoms of depression without healing the source of it.

As you can see, there are a variety of causes for depression and any one of them can trigger a depressive event.

When someone says they're depressed, believe them. It's not just their imagination. It's their reality and they are reaching out for help.

> The world leans on us. When we sag, the whole world seems to droop.
> Eric Hoffer, (1902 - 1983),
> American author, philosopher.

Often, a depressed person will withdraw from a partner. Ashamed of their predicament and not knowing how to cope, they tend to curl up within themselves. Talking about the sorrow can often help release it but the deeper the depression the harder it is to put into words. This can be hard on a relationship because often the partner feels left out in the cold, not knowing how or even what they need to do to help the depressed partner cope.

> Sorrow is easy to express and so hard to tell.
> Joni Mitchell,
> Canadian folk singer.

The Talking Stick is one of the most effective ways to encourage the slow emergence of deep-rooted emotions at the core of the depression. Through uninterrupted and continuous verbal expression, the Talking Stick gives a person the opportunity to emotionally backtrack and find the root causes of their depression. Something as simple as a Talking Stick can trigger a release of repressed feelings which is powerful enough to transform a person's emotional state of being. Frequently, enormous amounts of stored feelings contribute to depression. The use of the Talking Stick can assist you in safely releasing those feelings by verbally expressing them in free flow until your emotions are emptied.

The Talking Stick, using Method 2, works well in a therapeutic setting with a professional counselor assisting you or your partner in gently letting go of deep feelings. However, it can be equally as effective if you choose to assist your partner in releasing feelings using the Talking Stick. It's important that you're prepared to experience overwhelming emotion from them. If you feel you're not up to it then by all means seek out a counselor who is capable of facilitating your partner. If you still would like to listen to your partner's feelings, it's important to allow your partner the space to express whatever feelings may arise without you trying to '"fix" them by giving advice. All your partner needs you to do is just listen without judgment. The best gift that you can bestow upon your partner is to listen with ears of compassion.

> Where there is sorrow there is holy ground.
> Oscar Wilde, (1856 - 1900),
> British author playwright

As partners in a relationship, together you can walk the path back to emotional wellbeing. Through knowledge, mutual love and compassion, ultimately both of you will be greatly enriched by the sorrows overcome.

> Life was never meant to be a struggle; just a gentle progression from one point to another, much like walking through a valley on a sunny day.
> Stuart Wilde, British born,
> American author of The Sixth Sense.

Chapter 14

Romance and Recreation

Keep love in your heart. A life without it is like a sunless garden when the flowers are dead. The consciousness of loving and being loved brings a warmth and richness to life that nothing else can bring.
Oscar Wilde, (1854 - 1900),
Irish author.

There are many reasons why the strong flow of romance between a couple often diminishes to a trickle over time. Stress, career and the responsibility of raising children are certainly a few of the reasons why romance dwindles. However, the primary reason for a lack of romance in a long-term relationship is laziness.

When both of you were trying to win the other's love, you each put lots of effort and attention into making things fun and romantic. You were constantly thinking of creative ways you could spend time together such as dancing, intimate dinners, movies, etc.

You probably couldn't get enough of each other. You wanted to make sure that your partner thought you were interesting, intelligent and exciting. Certainly, you both wanted to present yourselves in the best possible light.

What happened to the days of wine and roses?

After the initial romantic phase, you probably both started taking each other for granted and stopped putting in the effort. Familiarity crept in and you came to the mistaken conclusion that you knew everything about each other. Nothing could be further from the truth because a human being is a multi-faceted condensation of pure life energy with a complexity and depth of individuality that would take you 20 lifetimes to truly recognize. You just haven't been paying attention to each other. You know the obvious parts of each other's personality but what you haven't searched for is the exquisite subtleties of the person you're sharing a bed with.

See each other with fresh eyes

Every human being is a diamond in the rough with many unexplored facets awaiting our discovery. As we grow in character and start expressing more of our individuality, we are able to uncover and polish our newly-found facets and allow them to shine forth in our life. Potentially, if both partners in an intimate relationship are growing on all levels – physically, spiritually, mentally and emotionally – they would constantly be seeing each other anew every day. There would always be some new aspect of yourselves emerging which would keep the other thoroughly interested.

The allure of affairs

One of the most tempting aspects of an affair is that the person who is attracted to you sees you with fresh eyes. The person does not view you as a mother, father, housecleaner or gardener. As a potential lover, you are viewed in a sexual, romantic, and mysterious way. If there's been a long drought in the romance department at home, then any attention like this would feel like the long-awaited monsoons have arrived.

When your partner has been neglectful of your romantic needs and desires, it can feel overwhelming and irresistible to feel desired by another individual outside of your relationship. Many unnecessary affairs occur because individuals are thirsty for attention, appreciation and romance.

Keeping the fires of passion and romance well stoked within your relationship can go a long way toward preventing any unnecessary attractions from coming into your lives.

Recreation vs responsibility

You and your partner came together for one primary reason — recreation. You wanted to have fun together, enjoy hot sex, share the joys of life and have a true playmate at your side.

You did not come together in a relationship with the primary intention of being responsible. You didn't look deeply into each other eyes and say, "My darling, I so look forward to our future years of exhausting joint responsibility for three children, massive educational debt, a crippling home mortgage, two car loans, physical and emotional fatigue, boredom, two dogs, one cat, and taking care of our elderly parents in their twilight years." It's safe to say if you had a crystal ball showing you this picture, instead of asking each other for a commitment, you would have committed yourself to the nearest mental hospital and pleaded with them to lock you up until you came to your senses.

You came together for recreation not responsibility

Yes we all have responsibilities and that's part of life. It's just that if you have the responsibilities without the recreation and romance, life becomes very dull indeed. It's vital for the health of your union, not to mention your own physical and emotional health, to reawaken the recreation part of your relationship by pumping some fun and romance into it while it still has a pulse.

Ideas for enhancing romance and recreation

Clear withholds – If you and your partner are accumulating a lot of emotional withholds such as anger and disappointment, you certainly won't be interested in any kind of romance. When you're each feeling resentments toward each other, the last thing you'll want to do is to make love by candlelight after taking a long bath together. After all, who wants to sleep with the enemy? It's impossible to feel deep levels of love when you are harboring stagnant emotions against each other.

Before planning any fun events, start clearing any unexpressed emotions that you're withholding from each other by using the Talking Stick. As your emotional reservoir starts emptying, you'll notice feelings of warmth begin to surface toward your partner. Continuing to clear withholds on a regular basis will free up positive feelings that you both can express on the dance floor.

Plan regular dates – You will always find the time to do the things you love to do. If you value spending time alone with your partner on a romantic date, you'll always be able to create the time to do so. There is no excuse for you and your partner not to date each other on a regular basis. Even if you have 10 children and zero money, you still can find the time and energy to go out on a weekly date with your partner if you truly want to.

Ideally, you can at least go out one evening a week to a movie or a dinner together without the kids. You owe it to yourself and your relationship to plan your dates by writing them down in your calendar. It doesn't have to cost a lot of money, because the most important thing is for you and your partner to spend valuable time together away from home. After all, how much does it cost to sit in the park and watch the sunset together? What will it cost you if you both neglect enjoying regular fun and romantic outings as a part of your relationship? The ultimate cost may be numbing boredom, passionless interactions and even perhaps the eventual dissolution of your relationship. Once or twice a week, save your dinner for after the children's bedtime. After they're sleeping, prepare yourself a romantic candlelight dinner for you and your partner. Prepare the food together or alternate cooking meals for each other.

At least once a month, take pleasure in an overnight stay at a hotel together or drop the children off at the relatives, and you go home for a night all to yourselves.

When time and circumstances allow, arrange holidays of longer duration for just you and your partner and leave the kids at home with the relatives. Even a short one-week trip away can be incredibly bonding for both of you. Shared travel is exciting because it takes you away from your usual home routine and acts as an aphrodisiac for your relationship.

Parents often use children as a convenient excuse for not getting away together by themselves. Keep family holidays totally separate events from you and your partner's romantic excursions away. There is absolutely no need to feel any guilt about leaving the kids at home. Just because everyone else in the neighborhood is willing to sacrifice the health of their relationship by refusing to "abandon" their children doesn't mean that you have to buy into some illusory ideal of always keeping the family together. You work very hard at taking care of your children, so regularly scheduled trips away are thoroughly well deserved. Who says that you have to wait until you're retired and the children off on their own before you and your partner get to spend holidays together? It's your life and you are free to arrange your time any way you see fit.

Before you know it, the joint effort to infuse your relationship with some fun and excitement will cause you to see each other through romantic eyes again.

Enjoy physical recreation together – We live in a physical body and yet in our sedentary culture we often forget to get it moving through some form of exercise, and our health eventually suffers as a result. Simple things like walking on the beach together or gentle hikes in the woods can serve to reduce stress while sharing some form of outdoor recreation in each other's company. You spend way too much time indoors under artificial lights or in front of television and computer screens absorbing life-negating radiation. Getting outdoors together while breathing fresh air and enjoying the views will add a fun new element to your relationship while giving you the benefits of regular physical exercise.

Re-create your bodies

Another benefit of exercise is the toning and reshaping of your body. Barring some physical disability, it's never too late for both of you to choose to shape up. It's a lot easier if you mutually commit to a joint exercise program. There isn't an ideal body shape, as we all come in various packages and sizes. Unfortunately, many people's personal obsession about their bodies has created a legacy of eating disorders and an overemphasis on physical perfection. The other side of the coin are individuals who have allowed their bodies to become unhealthy with poor nutritional choices and an overall lack of exercise. It's not about obsessive physical perfection nor is it about totally neglecting bodily needs. It's about finding the physical balance that's right for you. You know the proper weight and muscle tone that feels good to you. You don't have to be obsessive about exercise but one of the greatest gifts you can give to your partner is an attractive body. Sure, it takes work and commitment to ensure that you will stay healthy and fit throughout your lifetime but is there anything more valuable than radiant health? When you feel healthy and fit, you feel sexy and attractive. Sharing physical recreation together like hiking, weight training, yoga or tai chi can improve your health while enjoying fun in the sun at the same time.

Surprise, surprise – We all love surprises. Creatively generating surprises for your partner at every opportunity adds life and passion to your relationship. Surprising your partner shows them that you're thinking about them and are willing to put the effort in to make them feel special and appreciated. Make birthday and anniversary celebrations special by adding the element of surprise to the event. The best surprises are the ones that we don't expect. It doesn't have to be big, expensive surprises. Thoughtful small surprises work just as effectively.

For example, after a hard day at the office you're leaving for the dreaded ride home in traffic when your partner greets you outside with babysitters arranged and tickets in hand to your favorite theatre. Another example is that you've recently become aware of your partner's physical and emotional exhaustion from overwork so you arrange to have a massage therapist waiting to surprise him when he arrives home from work. When watching television together you can surprise your partner by soaking their feet in hot water and then giving a massage with scented oils. Just get creative because the list of possible ways to surprise your partner is endless.

> The husband who decides to surprise his wife is often very much surprised himself.
> Voltaire, (1694 – 1778),
> French historian, writer.

Thinking of ways to surprise your partner creates excitement and joy for yourself as well. It's fun to see the surprised look on your partner's face when you present them with your thoughtful act. Continually surprising each other keeps your relationship always fresh and in romantic mode and will go a long way toward sustaining passion and excitement in your relationship.

Chapter 15

Closing Ceremonies

Don't be dismayed at good-byes. A farewell is necessary before you can meet again. And meeting again, after moments or lifetimes, is certain for those who are friends.
Richard Bach, (1936 -),
American author.

There are no guarantees in life. You cannot guarantee how many more breaths you will take, tomorrow's weather or the length of time remaining in your relationship. It's a truth most of us feel very uncomfortable in facing. We know in the back of our mind that nothing in time and space lasts forever and yet it's not the type of thought that we like to entertain consciously. Out of fear and an attempt to lock things in, we vow to remain at each other's side for the rest of our lives. It creates a false sense of security because, in truth, the only reason two individuals choose to remain with each other in a relationship is the bonds of love and not two ink-dried signatures on a piece of paper. Even if the goal is to remain in your relationship for the rest of your life, eventually one of you is going to check out of this hotel called Earth, so to speak, and leave the relationship. At that moment, if you are the partner left behind, should you be awarded a special medal for going the distance? Perhaps you should and perhaps not.

There are no failures, just experiences

Statistics vary, but on average between 40 and 50 percent of marriages end in divorce. That means that 50 to 60 percent of marriages remain intact. Many people will argue that to divorce is a mistake. The question must be asked: What percentage of the people remaining together in their marriages are actually the ones who are making a mistake?

You can make a mistake in mathematics but not in relationships. In relationships, you make choices. Sometimes those choices turn out to be painful and you may consider them a mistake when in actuality they are just a growth experience of life. Each of us makes the best possible choices in relationships given our awareness at the time. Why should anyone else judge you or you judge yourself when it comes to your relationship decisions?

'Till our life lessons are over do us part

Referring back to the basic premise of this book, we are primarily here on Earth to learn the lessons of love. In my experience, it's a reality I know to be true. No spiritual power is trying to hurt you by hooking you up with a person who causes you pain in life. If you have experienced difficulties and pain in your relationships, it is only because of conscious and unconscious choices made by you. If you resist learning your lessons and choose to remain unconscious, you can expect many of your lessons to be hard ones. It's like sailing a ship with no rudder. The reef awaits you. As you learn your lessons of love, more harmony will manifest in your relationships.

Your consciousness, soul, spirit, higher self or whatever you want to call it, is continually attracting relationship patterns which will help you to expand your ability to give and receive love. Darwin was partially correct. As human beings, we not only evolve physically and mentally but we also evolve emotionally. It's through the heart, or feelings, that we are able to merge with the beloved. As a species, we are rapidly developing the increased ability to experience higher vibratory feelings of ecstasy and bliss. Before being able to enjoy these states of being, we must first purify our heavier emotions by transforming feelings of anger, fear and sorrow into their higher emotional equivalents of tranquility, trust and joy.

This transformation takes place in the furnace of your relationships. It's made through the interactions of self to self where the rough edges of your human personality are sanded away to reveal the brilliant facets of your spiritual individuality. Your higher self knows your next relationship lesson and will attract those individuals which can assist you in learning that lesson. As long as there are lessons to be learned, the energetic bond which holds the relationship together will remain intact. These lessons may last a lifetime together. If, however, your relationship lessons are over and you both have exhausted the possibilities of learning from each other, the bond that held your union together dissolves and you are free to move on to your next lesson.

If you look at the area of friendships, there are people in your past who are no longer in your life, but at one time you were extremely close to. It's just that your life lessons were over with that friend so you gradually drifted apart. Some of your friends are still with you because there are more lessons to learn from each other. If you and a close friend of many years chose to part ways, does that mean that you had a failed friendship? It's the same with intimate relationships. If you and your partner choose to end your marriage, how dare anyone judge you by pronouncing your relationship a failed marriage!

Longevity in a relationship is not the only test of the quality of the partnership. In fact, many people remain in dreary, unrewarding relationships long past their "use by date." Length of time in a relationship does not automatically equate to a fulfilling union. Is a 30-year marriage between two people who barely relate to one another better than a five-year relationship where two individuals connected on many levels but then chose to separate because they were growing in different directions?

"I'm sorry it didn't work out!"

Has anyone said those words to you before? I remember someone saying them to me upon learning my former relationship had just ended.

"Des, I'm sorry it didn't work out for you and Patricia," she said. "What do you mean it didn't work out?" I replied.

"You know...your marriage failed," she responded.

I exclaimed, "Oh! You mean that because we didn't stay together until the end of our lives, traditional society judges my marriage to be a failure. Yes, compared to those expectations I guess my marriage wasn't a success. However, what if society is wrong? What if Patricia and I were successful in learning the lessons we needed from each other? After all, we both grew enormously from our time together. We brought two beautiful young daughters into the world. We learned how to take care of our physical bodies and become healthier. Patricia's love cracked open the walls around my heart and I learned how to receive. Together we explored spiritual concepts which opened our minds to truth. It's true we only spent seven years together and our relationship didn't last a lifetime. We had our share of difficulties and painful experiences to overcome and our communications skills were certainly not developed. Was our relationship a failure? Of course not."

Till death do us part?

There is an assumption in our culture that a successful marriage or partnership is one that lasts a lifetime. Anything less is a failure. Until recently, there was enormous shame attached to individuals who divorced. Now, it's still looked down upon by society but there's not nearly the level of disgrace associated with it a century ago.

It's true that a couple of generations ago, relationships tended to last for a longer period than today. Most families have a myth about how wonderfully happy their grandparents or great-grandparents were in their 50-year marriage. Some of these relationships were truly happy but I think that the great majority of partners were in an endurance contest and didn't really experience great levels of joy. Because survival was more difficult than today, when choosing a partner practicalities prevailed over emotional fulfillment. If they were unhappy in their relationship they often didn't choose the option of leaving because of the social stigma attached to divorce. They remained in the relationship and suffered their sorrows in silence. The only thing for which they had bragging rights was how long they were able to put up with each other.

On the other hand, if you and your partner are clearly communicating, growing, expanding and learning together, the longer you are together, the greater the potential for a stronger and richer experience of intimacy.

Longevity in a relationship can lead to deeper intimacy

Sure, you can enjoy a powerful relationship with someone you have only have been with for a few years. It's just that you need the element of time to reveal each other's depths of being. With the benefit of time, you each discover and enjoy various unexplored facets of each other's individuality which greatly enriches your mutual lives. A greater depth of intimacy is possible because of a longer length of time spent together.

Today, people are much more interested in a richer quality of life in their relationships. More and more people are on the path of personal growth and there is the general expectation that an intimate relationship should be fulfilling on many levels. There is less patience for remaining in a relationship which is less than rewarding.

> Leaving a relationship when it is not in your best interest to depart is just as destructive as remaining in a relationship when it is not in your best interest to stay.
>
> Des Coroy.

This recent cultural reluctance to stay in an unhappy partnership is both positive and negative. The positive aspect is that people are no longer willing to waste their lives in a lifeless relationship which cannot be resuscitated. The negative aspect is that many individuals leave their relationship without giving each other the opportunity to regenerate the partnership. They may have given up too soon.

Should I stay or should I go?

One of the specific intentions of this book is to prevent you and your partner from abandoning ship too soon. The communication techniques presented within are designed to help you gain clarity on whether or not you are both rowing in the same direction. Communicating with the safety of the Talking Stick can help you and your partner discover if you both want to continue walking on the same life path. You owe it to yourselves, your relationship and, if there are any, your children to be as clear as you can be about such an important decision as a final separation.

Communicating with each other at a time when most people are withdrawing takes character and courage to stay engaged in constructive dialogue. Of course, it takes two people to communicate effectively because you can't do it on your own. A partner refusing to communicate about such an important issue could be a deciding confirmation about their unwillingness to participate in the relationship.

Another intention of this book is to assist you and your partner in gaining clarity as to whether it's in your highest good to remain together in your relationship. If you and your partner have attentively worked with the concepts in this book, you have gained valuable insights into the viability and health of your relationship.

Answering the following questions may again serve to remind you of what you have discovered about your relationship. If you answer no to any of these questions, ask yourself if there is potential to change it to a yes in the near future.

Does your relationship expectation list match up? Do you both value and speak the truth?
Do you each listen more effectively to the other? Are you now fighting fairly in your relationship?
Are you using the Talking Stick with each other to assist in improving your listening and communication skills?
Do you feel safe enough to speak about anything to your partner?
Are you clearing emotional withholds with each other?
Do you share the financial, domestic and parental responsibilities more equally?
Are you each willing to take responsibility for any mirroring between each other and to let go of blame?
Are you willing to forgive each other for any past transgressions and let it go once and for all?
Are you having more fun with each other?

If you and your partner have answered no to most of these questions with very little chance of turning them into a yes, then you may be at a completion point in your union and are moving onto separate paths. If either one of you continues to refuse to work on the issues of your relationship, then I have one more question for you.

At the end of your life experience on Earth, when you look back and remember the time you are now immersed in, will you regret remaining in an unfulfilling relationship and settling for less love than you deserve?

Deciding on whether you should remain in your relationship is one of the most important decisions you will ever make. It's one that only you and your partner can ultimately determine, no matter what amount of well-meaning advice is offered by others. Because it's often a time of confusion, it's difficult not to be influenced by the opinions of family and friends. If you're depending on another to make the choice for you, you're asking for serious trouble. Considering the lack of real joy in most relationships, I'd be very suspicious of the source of any free pearls of wisdom thrown your way.

If after reading and working with the concepts in this book, you still haven't reached the mental clarity needed to make the right choice, I strongly recommend utilizing the services of a professional relationship counselor. A counselor can assist you and your partner in clarifying the issues confronting you in your relationship. Breakthroughs can often be achieved in understanding what the proper path is for both of you to take. If you have resistance to attending counseling because you're afraid of revealing your feelings and may consider it weak to do so, just remember that a truly strong individual knows how to reach out for help when needed. When your car breaks down you need a professional mechanic and when your partnership breaks down you need a relationship specialist.

Counseling creates clarity

It's important when entering any therapeutic counseling that you are both committed to the communication process involved or it won't work. Make a firm mutual commitment to attend as many sessions as necessary until greater understanding is achieved. You're there to listen to each other and to express your viewpoints in safety. You're not there to necessarily save your relationship because you may discover that you want to part ways.

If you both truly participate in the sessions, you will gain greater clarity on the health of your relationship and the possibilities of regenerating it. Because sensitive emotions will be uncovered, there may be a tendency for one of you to withdraw from the counseling process. It's important for both of you to resist disengaging from your sessions by persevering with your commitment.

If you decide that it's in your best interest to dissolve the bonds of your relationship, at the very least you will know within your heart that you did not walk away from it without giving it one more attempt at healing any rifts between you and your partner. At a minimum, you will both learn ways of parting gracefully. You will also gain coping skills for dealing with any possible anger or sorrow that may arise in the future. If there are children involved, it's vital that you seek support on how to deal with the various emotional ups and downs of shared responsibilities with the kids. Learning from a professional counselor how to protect your children from any negative consequences of your separation is very important to their emotional health and will make a huge difference to their future happiness.

Even if your partner refuses to attend counseling sessions, it's still in your best interest to seek assistance for yourself in learning how to cope with a challenging emotional situation. There are many competent relationship counselors who can assist you.

It's essential when selecting a relationship counselor that you both feel very comfortable with the person chosen. If one of you doesn't feel safe with a particular counselor, consider the possibility of choosing another. There is a natural tendency to attempt to get the counselor to side with you in any disagreement with your partner, but doing so will only create distrust in your partner and undermine the whole process. A competent professional counselor is objectively at the center point of the scales and their intention is to facilitate improved communication by mediating any tensions between you.

Request intuitive guidance

There is one more foolproof method of knowing for sure if it's in your best interest to remain in your relationship. In the past, whenever I have been confused about what to do in my relationship, when my back was up against the wall and I didn't know where to turn, I relaxed, let go of my frantic mental gymnastics and turned within for the unerring guidance from my Higher Self.

Your Higher Self is always waiting to lead you toward your higher good. Whatever name you want to call it according to your beliefs, Great Spirit, Universe, Jesus, God/Goddess, Buddha, Infinite Intelligence, Allah, Universal Law, Shiva, Divine Love, Yahweh, Higher Self, or Creator, this Higher Self of yours knows exactly which path is best for you to take in your relationship.

Your Higher Self communicates to you through your intuition. Intuition is your infallible guidance system connecting you directly to Infinite Intelligence, the cosmic programmer of the Universe. This Infinite Intelligence is continually guiding you toward your highest possible good in every moment and situation of your existence.

Your intuition speaks to you in subtle feelings or flashes of insight which create a sense of inner knowing. Coming directly from Infinite Intelligence, it is always accurate. Your logical mind is good at analyzing situations but it is often incorrect in its conclusions. Your logical mind is a computer and your intuition is the programmer. The key to discerning whether it's your logical mind or your intuition is in the immediate time after making any decision.

If there is still a slight feeling of unease or fear that you made the wrong decision, then it is probably your logical mind choosing and not your intuition. If your intuition has guided you to make a decision, you will experience a feeling of peace and wellbeing with that decision. Instead of anxiousness, you will feel relaxed along with an inner knowledge that you made the right choice. The more you practice discerning the difference between your logical mind and your intuitive mind, the easier it will be to tap into the universal guidance of your intuition at will for the benefit of making decisions in your day-to-day life. If you want to know beyond the shadow of a doubt whether you should remain in your relationship or move on, then you have to request guidance from your Higher Self. Every time in my life when I was in a crisis of indecision and I used this simple request for direction, I received clear guidance within days of asking for it.

As simple as this may seem, the key to receiving guidance from your Higher Self is to ask for it. Your logical mind likes control. To your logical mind, if it can't find a solution, there must not be one. Intuition has information of which your logical mind is not aware. In this free will universe, the only way your Higher Self can assist you is if you freely ask for its support. Intuition overrides your analytical mind and speaks straight to your heart. Create a request for guidance in your own words.

You're welcome to use mine if it feels right to you. If you're an atheist, use the term Higher Mind if you feel more comfortable because you will still get a response to your request.

1. Find a private place and relax – Take a walk on the beach or in nature or find a private quiet space at home. Center yourself by relaxing and going within.

2. Ask for guidance – Think of your indecision about your relationship, and when it feels right to you let words similar to these come from your heart: *"Great Spirit, if it's in our highest good to remain together in our relationship, then please give us an answer and guide us both to a positive breakthrough in our relationship. And Great Spirit, if it's not in our highest good to remain together in our relationship, then please give us an answer and assist us in gracefully releasing each other with love."* Allow any feelings to surface which may be present. When releasing this prayer request to your Higher Self, it's important to let go of all attachment to any particular result you may want.

Your conscious mind may desire an outcome which may be in opposition to what your Higher Self desires for you and your partner. Surrender your will to your Higher Self and be willing to accept the guidance even if it's not what your logical mind wants to hear. Consciously, you have a limited view, while your Higher Self sees the total view and is always seeking to guide you toward your greater good. You'll know if you have surrendered by the sense of release that you will feel. Let it go for now and go on with your life fully trusting that your Higher Self will bring you an answer to your request.

In my own life, when faced with the choice of whether I should remain in a relationship or not, the following short prayer always worked for me. "If she's meant for me than let it be, if not, then let it stop". As simple as this little request for guidance might seem to be, it's also very powerful. Every time I have truly released the relationship to my Higher Self, I received a clear answer, although sometimes it may not have been what a part of me wanted. If my intuition guided me to let go of the relationship, then I learned to trust that my greater good would manifest by following another path of love. And if the guidance was to remain in the union, then I would know in my heart that the best path for me was to continue putting all of my effort and love into the relationship.

The keys to successfully following your intuition are to let go of wanting to control the outcomes, release any specific expectations and to totally trust the answers which will come from your intuition or Higher Self.

3. Expect an answer – Pay attention to your hunches or feelings over the next few days and at some point you will have a sense and an awareness of which path is best for you. You will just know. If you're still stressed out about your choice then it's probably not your intuition, so just relax and wait for your answer. Your intuition speaks to you in subtle ways. It's like fine tuning your listening to hear the sound of the train traveling in the far distance. At some point, you will experience a sense of peace and an inner resolution of your dilemma. Be willing to trust the response.

Staying together for the children

One of the primary reasons partners choose to remain in their relationship is for the sake of their children. It's a very difficult choice to make because doing what's best for the children is a fundamental concern. Deciding whether it's in your children's best interest for you to remain in a marriage will be a unique decision for you based on the complexities of your relationship. Remaining in your relationship for a period of time may create the stability necessary for your children's need for security.

However, if you and your partner are experiencing ongoing tension and a lack of joy in your partnership, then the damage done to your children's wellbeing may be far greater if you remain in your relationship than if you leave. It's not always in your children's interest to superglue your relationship together when the best choice may be to allow the relationship to naturally break apart.

Separating for the children

If your relationship is beyond the point of repair and the only reason you and your partner are remaining in your union is for the children, it's important that you closely evaluate how your children are handling your decision. The tension and lack of love between you and your partner may be a burden too heavy for your children to bear.

Even at a young age, children are extremely switched on and they readily perceive any underlying currents within your relationship. You may think that you are adept at keeping the relationship difficulties with your partner separate from your children but, even with your best intentions, your kids perceive everything on a feeling level.

Children are emotionally sensitive creatures who have an unerring radar system for seeing through you and your partner's attempts at propping up the false façade of the happy family. In addition, children learn by example and the lesson you are teaching them is, "When you get to be an adult and you marry someone you're not compatible with, you too can remain in a dispassionate, loveless relationship for your children!" Is that what you want your kids to experience in their future?

Would you counsel your son or daughter to sacrifice joy, passion and any possibility of fulfilment for the sake of their future children? I don't think so, but if you remain in your relationship for the wrong reason that's exactly the lesson they are learning.

Especially when children are involved, many people believe that a marriage should be saved at all costs. I strongly disagree with this viewpoint. Sure, you can force the issue and attempt to resuscitate your relationship by keeping it on the artificial life support of apathy. You may keep it alive for a while but at the cost of your integrity and happiness. Why should a couple stay in a relationship if they have absolutely no chance of being happy together and their children are suffering as a result?

You are free to decide

After careful consideration, if you have arrived at a decision to separate, you have every right to do so. Do not let anyone interfere in your freedom as a human being to make choices in your life which you feel are in your best interests. Your time is your own. You have complete freedom to choose whom you would like to spend it with. No one has a right to demand from you one second more of your life if you don't want to give it. Don't let the pressures of religion, family, or friends force you to remain in a relationship that you think is not in your highest good. If you're coming from your integrity and you're not trying to hurt anyone, it's perfectly okay to dissolve the bonds of your relationship.

Letting go with love

If you and your partner have finally come to the end of your life travels together, then this next section will assist you in saying your goodbyes with grace.

Usually, it's difficult to unravel your life from another's when there are strong ties that keep you both entangled. Partners can be linked financially, emotionally, physically, and the strongest link of all, children. Under the best circumstances, separating from your partner can still be an emotionally draining undertaking. Unfortunately, in our non-emotional culture, a relationship break-up provides one of life's acceptable outlets for such volatile emotions as rage and revenge and so out it pours. Because of this potential pressure, it's important to minimize the amount of stress experienced in the separation process.

Some things are beyond your control, such as the reaction of family and friends to your impending parting, or the emotional response from your partner. However, you do have control over your own mental and emotional attitude toward your separation. A balanced and positive mental approach to the changes which lie ahead is your greatest protection against adversity. Viewing things from a higher perspective will assist you in avoiding the traps of blame.

Burst the bubble of blame

You have a choice of two possible roads in front of you. The low road is a path chosen by most people and it leads to bitterness, blame, victimhood and revenge. Your other choice is taking the high road, which is a path traveled by few. It leads to understanding, compassion, forgiveness and renewal. The choice is yours. Which road will you choose?

The following points are a list of practical suggestions which will assist you in reducing the levels of stress while experiencing the process of your separation:

Avoid self-judgment – Separation or divorce often brings up feelings of failure, regret and guilt. "If only I had put more effort into the relationship," is a common self judgment that occurs but that's not the only reason why your relationship is ending. Perhaps you could have put more effort into the relationship; however, you have learned the lesson to participate more in a future partnership. There are two individuals in your relationship and both of you share responsibility for what occurred between you no matter how guilty you may feel. The last thing you need now is to give yourself a hard time by overanalyzing your past actions within the relationship. Learn from your misjudgments and grow from them but please don't beat yourself up anymore. There doesn't have to be any blame laid on yourself or your partner. Remember, we're all learning the lessons of love and maybe the only reason you are parting ways is because class is over between you.

> Let's not burden our remembrance with a heaviness that's gone.
>
> William Shakespeare, (1564 – 1616),
> British poet, playwright, actor.

Avoid blaming your partner – It doesn't matter if it was primarily your decision to leave the relationship or your partner's choice, it's so tempting to play the blame game. Many times a partner will hold on to his or her resentment and blame for years, thinking that by doing so they will somehow get even with the partner who hurt them. The only person who's going to suffer if you continue to carry judgment or anger toward your former partner is you. Your former partner will move on with life but your anger will simmer inside until it eventually has a destructive effect on your emotional and physical health. It's in your best interests to let go of your judgments and move on as soon as possible. By attempting to offload the responsibility for the breakup of your relationship onto your partner, you avoid taking any personal responsibility yourself.

Break out the violins, because you're about to play a beautiful rendition of that all-time classic victim's song, "Woe, woe is me!" Playing the victim is not very flattering anymore. With the growing divorce rate today, believe me, your friends are running low on sympathy. They have heard all the stories anyway so don't bore them with: "She left me for another man," or "He left me for another man," or "She kicked me out of the house and it was Christmas," or "He had an affair with the barmaid who worked at the pub where he gambled all of our money away!" If men and women only knew how judgmental it sounded to others, they would quit blaming their partner for all of the problems in the relationship. If you can't control your tongue and you need to speak to someone about how wronged you were, pay a professional counselor to listen to your story.

I've always been careful about pointing the finger of blame

at a former partner because it begs the question, what am I complaining about since I'm the one that chose her as a partner in the first place. Remembering that like attracts like, as repellent as this thought may be, you obviously carry some of the same character traits as the partner you are judging. You and your partner had various lessons to learn about love or you would not have been together, however miserable your relationship may have been. There are no accidents in this universe. After your pain subsides, objectively determine what lesson you've learned from your partner and move on. Whether you are aware of it or not, your former partner has served you in some way. So please stop making them wrong because your judgment keeps you tied to the past.

> All blame is a waste of time. No matter how much fault you find with another, and regardless of how much you blame him, it will not change you. The only thing blame does is to keep the focus off you when you are looking for external reasons to explain your unhappiness or frustration. You may succeed in making another feel guilty about something by blaming him, but you won't succeed in changing whatever it is about you that is making you unhappy.
> Wayne Dyer, (1940 -),
> American psychotherapist, author, lecturer.

Don't expect complete support – Often, the people in your life that you expect to be the most supportive, won't be. Separation and divorce rattle the security of your family and friends. If it can happen to you, it can happen to anybody and that scares them. Don't be surprised if they turn on you by judging your decision as a mistake. Another common reason for people to desert you is the jealousy factor. They're envious of you separating from your partner because they haven't mustered the courage to leave their unhappy relationship. The individuals who judge you the most about ending your relationship are usually the ones who are most miserable in theirs.

Don't accept any negative judgments from the people in your life, especially if they are unsolicited. They are entitled to their point of view but they're not entitled to dump it on you when you really don't want to hear it. Tell them firmly that you appreciate their concern but that you would prefer not to hear their opinions any more. You need their support, not judgment. After all, what right do your family and friends have to criticize your decision when you're the one who had to sleep with your partner every night?

> They condemn what they do not understand.
> Marcus T. Cicero, (c. 106 – 43 BC),
> Great Roman orator, politician.

Prepare for lifestyle adjustments – In the great majority of separations, both partners will find it somewhat difficult at first to adjust to some of the lifestyle changes, which are inevitable.

Living expenses can sometime double because income is divided and you are now living in two residences. It doesn't have to be a permanent situation but it's more than likely you will experience some downturn in your day-to-day lifestyle. If children are involved, explain to them that everyone is going to have to tighten the belt for a while.

Don't worry about the children, as the situation is a character builder that teaches them how to handle adversity and setbacks in life. Even though it may be a little tough for a while financially, don't let money worries prevent you from leaving a relationship where you feel trapped.

For the privilege of freedom, many wealthy refugees have abandoned their riches and homeland to escape a repressive political situation. If you're in an awful relationship with no possibility of renewal, don't let material comforts and money prevent you from making your dash to freedom. Your distaste for driving a less expensive car or living in a more modest residence is no reason to sell your soul by remaining in a lifeless union.

> Life belongs to the living, and he who lives must
> be prepared for changes.
> Johann Wolfgang Von Goethe, (1749 – 1832),
> German poet, dramatist, novelist.

Let go of your fear of being alone – Even if you are miserable in your relationship, you may fear being able to find another partner as mediocre as the one you have now. Your fear of being alone may be so overwhelming that it keeps you immobilized in your current relationship. If you decide to leave the relationship and you do have some time living alone, enjoy it! Some of my most enjoyable years on Earth have been when I was not in a relationship because it gave me the opportunity to explore many of my own needs and desires. I learned that my self-worth was not predicated on me being in a relationship. Society puts enormous pressure on you to be in a relationship and to fall in love. Don't worry about the rush to fall in love again or whether you will do better next time. Instead, learn to fully love yourself to the point where you are radiating love to others. Therefore, instead of seeking to fall in love, just "be love" and people will always want to fall in love with you!

> You cannot be lonely if you like the person you're
> alone with.
> Wayne Dyer, (1940 –),
> American psychologist, author, lecturer.

Keep your children out of it – Under no circumstances are you to emotionally harm the children entrusted to your care by unloading onto them the rage and sorrow you're carrying toward your former partner. Your children will have enough difficulty in this life without you adding to their emotional burden because you couldn't restrain yourself from trying to hurt your former partner by involving your children.

WARNING: When one parent unloads toxic resentments

about a former partner onto a child, the impact of that action will deeply wound the child's heart. It's an emotional act of terror, which will have a devastating impact on a child's life. The child will be emotionally scarred for a long time. It is one of the most selfish and immature acts a human being can do to a child. If you find yourself in a situation where your anger is overwhelming toward your former partner and it's spilling over onto your children, stop doing it immediately and start cleaning up the damage you have done by setting the record straight with your children. Get professional help if necessary. Just because you or your former partner choose to remain sulking in your self-pity and rage, it doesn't give you the right to use your children as an emotional pawn to hurt your former partner. If you won't stop for your children's' sake, at least think about your own interests because karmically, whatever amount of negative hatred you channel through your children, the universe will return it back to you tenfold.

Don't emotionally lean on your children either by spilling your grief onto their little hearts. They're not equipped to handle the sorrow that you may share with them. Resist using your children as an emotional stand-in for the partner who is no longer in your life. No matter how angry you are with your former partner, avoid saying anything negative to the children about him or her. If the children are having a rough time coping with the changes, don't hesitate to enlist the support of a professional counselor for them, as it could make all the difference to their future happiness. Ideally, you and your partner should sit down with the children, when they are of an appropriate age, and explain to them that sometimes in life people just grow apart and that no one is to blame, especially them.

For the sake of your children's emotional well-being, please cease all hostilities with your partner before your children become hostile with you.

Des Coroy.

If possible, mediate, compromise, and negotiate everything – Attorneys are very effective at protecting your interests when you need them. It's just that they are expensive hired guns to be used only when necessary. Being paid by the hour, both legal teams benefit financially from conflict between you and your partner. It's to your mutual benefit to compromise on issues out-of-court and it's to the lawyers' benefit to encourage all-out war. Of course, we know they would never do such a thing! You and your partner may have accumulated financial resources over a long time. It makes no sense whatsoever to give away $10,000-$50,000 to a perfect stranger just because you and your former partner are having a little tiff! Maintaining a stubborn attitude of revenge toward your former partner can cost you both a lot of money.

Five years from now when you look back at this time, you don't want to feel foolish for throwing away a down payment on a new home, do you? Of course, it takes two people to be willing to negotiate and that may not be the case for you. Then you may need to spend money with a lawyer to protect yourself. If you and your partner can stop hostilities and maintain an objective mental clarity, you will be able to negotiate your differences with a professional mediator if necessary. The greatest pain of separation and divorce takes place when matters get dragged out in the courts. Besides being financially draining to both of you, it is also mentally and emotionally exhausting. At least put out the white flag for a while until you can compromise and settle your differences. Above all, be fair with each other and you will feel good about yourselves down the road. It's the intelligent thing to do.

> Fools and obstinate people make lawyers rich.
> Proverb.

Keep your commitments to your children – It's very important that you each keep your commitments concerning residency and contact with your children. Your children need both of you more than ever at this time and it's important that you follow through on your promises. Avoid arguments in front of the children during contact exchanges. Whichever partner (at this time, men are far more responsible for paying child support than women) is responsible for paying child support for the children, it is important not to let anger toward your former partner cause you to neglect your responsibility to your children. It's important for you to distinguish between your anger at your former partner and your love and caring for your children.

If you refuse to pay, or hide your assets to reduce the level of your child support payments, your desire for revenge will hurt your children and your former partner, but your own personal integrity and self-esteem will also suffer as a result of your selfishness. One day you'll have to explain to your children the reason you neglected your financial responsibility to them as a parent. Look, I know sometimes it can be difficult to fulfil your financial responsibility to your children. If you begin a new family it's especially difficult to make ends meet. A single parent on their own with children is also difficult without your financial support. Take care of your children financially and you will give them a good start in life and feel good about living up to your responsibility as a parent. Anyone can be a sperm or egg donor, but fatherhood or motherhood must be earned.

> Your life works to the degree you keep your agreements.
>
> Werner Erhard,
> American entrepreneur.

Avoid reuniting because of guilt – Make sure that if you choose to reestablish your relationship with your former partner, you're doing so because you want to and not because of guilt. Avoid reconciling if the only reason you're reuniting is because you feel sorry for your former partner or if the pressure of guilt is pushing you to reconnect.

If you truly desire to be with your partner in a relationship again then go for it. It takes a lot of energy to initiate a separation and carry it through. If you were to return to the relationship only because you feel guilty for ending it, then you probably will be going through the whole separation process again. A former partner may use the children as leverage in order to pressure you to reunite the family. If the issues which caused you to end your relationship were not resolved, when you return to the relationship those same issues will be waiting for you again. Let love and not guilt be the motivating factor for any possible reunion.

Partners in time

You are born into this life alone and you will leave this life alone. In between, you meet a lot of interesting people along the way, with whom you spend varying amounts of time. In the early part of your life, you didn't have a lot of choice in who would share time with you. As you grew into a fully independent human being, you started expressing freedom of choice in your associations with different people. You have a certain amount of time allotted to you in your life span while here on Earth. By and large, you have the complete freedom to choose the individuals who will be your partners in time as long as those individuals also choose you.

Every moment we spend with another individual is a precious gift of immense worth, the shared gift of time.

Des Coroy.

More precious than gold, this extremely rare string of moments called time is your lifespan. People will share this precious commodity with you in various ways. Friendships, business associates, fellow students, children, parents, strangers and intimate partners all share varying lengths of time with you. Out of all of these possible fellow time travelers, our intimate relationships are the most powerful and life-changing connections of all. It's the one form of relationship where we merge with another being on all levels — spiritual, mental, emotional and physical. It's on the physical, sexual level where the distinction is made from the other forms of human interaction.

Love transmutes pain into love

We are just beginning to explore the powerful vibratory experience of human sexuality as a way of merging with the divine in each other. The physical experience of orgasm is amazing as a pure experience of pleasure on the physical plane but that is not its only purpose. The intense energies of an orgasm also stimulate you on a mental and emotional level. These energies act as a catalyst in moving heavier emotions to the surface of your awareness in order to be healed through the power of your mutual love. Unfortunately, no one has really prepared us for this purification process because not many people are even aware of it.

One of the main reasons intimate relationships can be so incredibly difficult is because your shared sexuality stimulates your emotional energy field with powerful waves of vibration which bring up any deeply repressed feelings of anger, sorrow, and fear, all at once. Not making the connection between sex and surfacing emotions, you usually start associating these feelings with the presence of your partner in life because you certainly weren't feeling them before. Accusations can fly and you are completely unaware of the greater purpose that's taking place in your life. In actuality, even though the pain begins to overshadow the love in your relationship, you each have bestowed a great gift on the other. You have helped each other, through the crucible of emotional interaction, heal your hearts of many deep-seated wounds. You may not have been conscious of the process at work within you, and often it probably felt more like a beating than a healing, but it still occurred regardless of your awareness.

If your time has come to an end with your present intimate partner, it's important to realize that you each served the other in many supportive ways of which you are unaware. Consciously you may consider them the enemy at this time but your soul knows better.

> *The only gift is a portion of thyself.*
> Ralph Waldo Emerson, (1803 – 1882),
> American poet, essayist.

At the beginning of your relationship, you experienced opening ceremonies of one kind or another. It's an important symbol which marks the beginning of your time together in a relationship.

If you were in a relationship where you were dating or living together, then your opening ceremony might have been the courting period or when you first moved in together. If you were married, then your opening ceremony was more formally expressed with the highly colorful setting of a marriage ceremony.

We always recognize the beginning of a relationship with some type of ceremony but we never end a relationship with one. Most of us like to just sneak away from it without calling too much attention to ourselves.

Actually, we do have a closing ceremony for a marriage. It's amazingly ironic that to begin a relationship a ceremony is conducted with the couple standing in front of an audience with all eyes focused on them. The couple signs legal documents with a person who has the power to officially unite the marriage. It's called a church or legal wedding ceremony.

Years later, to end a relationship, a ceremony is conducted with the couple standing in front of an audience with all eyes focused on them. The couple signs legal documents with a person who has the power to officially dissolve the marriage. It's called a courtroom divorce ceremony.

One of the primary reasons we don't acknowledge the completion of our relationships is because most of them end poorly. Usually there is some degree of sorrow or anger still lingering like a bad aftertaste. Many times the end of a relationship comes as a complete surprise to one of the partners and it may take a while for that partner to overcome the shock and disappointment.

Another reason we don't officially end relationships is because of a feeling of failure that it didn't last. If the societal ideal of a relationship is one which lasts a lifetime, then anything less is perceived to be an inferior experience.

Because society places such a heavy emphasis on protecting the sacred institution of marriage, you probably feel that it is necessary for you to have a water-tight reason for leaving your marriage, or your family and friends might not support you. In order to separate from a relationship, quite often you will expand the negative traits of your partner in order to justify leaving the relationship. It's actually far better for you to put up with the sting of your family and friends' rejection and disapproval of your separation than to lose your integrity in order to get their acceptance by weaving false tales about your partner.

When you try to validate your reasons for ending your union by making your partner the scapegoat for all the problems in the relationship, you automatically devalue any positive experiences between you as well. This makes it much more difficult to say your goodbyes to each other with a sense of appreciation, because of your temporary amnesia about anything good in your union. It's commonly accepted by most people that when you end a relationship it's usually done with bitterness, judgment and regret. Even so, it doesn't mean that you have to follow the human herd down the well-worn path of hostility toward your former partner. Please, resist trashing the memories of the time shared with your former partner no matter how hurt or how angry you are now. There is another way.

No matter how long you and your former partner chose to be together, you have shared your most precious commodity, your time. Have you thanked each other for your mutual gift of love?

Time is the coin of your life. It is the only coin you have, and only you can determine how it will be spent. Be careful lest you let other people spend it for you.
Carl Sandburg, (1878 – 1967), American poet.

Doesn't it feel a little strange to spend a great amount of time with another human being and then walk away without deeply acknowledging their contribution to your life? You laugh with them, fight with them, eat with them, kiss them, share your hopes and dreams with them, intensely dislike them, have children with them, bathe with them, make love with them, cuddle with them, travel with them, wish you never laid eyes on them, play with them, dance with them, cry with them, see the worst sides of them, see the best sides of them. Think about it; your experiences together weren't all unpleasant. However difficult it may have been for you in your relationship, your partner chose to give you a most precious commodity, their time. I'm sure being with you wasn't always a bed of roses for them either. Your former partner is not the devil incarnate, no matter how much you want to delude yourself into believing so.

Closing Ceremonies

Getting closure on your relationship is necessary for you to move on in your life unburdened by the baggage of the past. Close this chapter of your life by acknowledging to each other, if possible, or at least to your own self, the positive experiences and lessons of your relationship together.

The following are a few suggestions which may assist you in releasing your former relationships with love.

If each partner desires to participate – To get to a place of acknowledging each other's contribution to your individual lives, it's important to release any resentment that you may be holding from the past. The Resentment Release

Process in Chapter Ten will assist you in doing so. This will support both of you in transforming any feelings of anger by seeing the greater picture involved in your relationship. You're not ready to perform Closing Ceremonies if you're still harboring destructive emotions toward your former partner. Wait until the time when you are finally beyond resentment. Don't be concerned about rushing things as both of you may not be ready for quite some time. It may be a month, a year or a decade after the dissolution of your relationship before you are ready to give your gifts of gratitude. At some point, when both of you feel at peace with the past, arrange a time and a place where you can both meet in private. Get away from the city and find an environment like a seashore or mountaintop where the beauty of nature can surround you.

Before meeting, think deeply about the time spent together in your relationship, and make a list of all the gifts you received from your partner for which you are grateful. If you were in an emotionally or physically abusive relationship, it may be difficult for you to find any good in your former relationship. Even if the only lesson you learned is never to allow yourself to be in an abusive situation again, that alone is something to be grateful for. Note only the positive in your list, because you both know what the negative experiences were and you have forgiven each other anyway. Write down such items on a notepad line by line, including specific acts of kindness, things that you learned, times you were nurtured, times you laughed, days you played together, times shared with the children, places you travelled, times you loved, difficulties overcome, moments of joy, and complete your list by writing down all the qualities you admire and respect in your former partner. When you each have completed your list, arrange a rendezvous at your chosen location and perhaps prepare a little picnic and bring a nice bottle of champagne along with you.

When you arrive at your spot, each of you sit facing each other with your list in hand. Alternate speaking one tribute off your list at a time. Remember to express only the most positive thoughts and feelings of gratitude to each other.

Treat this ceremony with the same sense of reverence and

appreciation which both of you experienced at your opening ceremony, the wedding. When one of you is speaking, the other is truly listening with mind and heart to the gifts of appreciation which are being presented to you. Keep alternating back and forth until both of you complete your list of acknowledgments. It's usually a very emotional experience so please allow yourself the freedom to experience the beautiful range of feelings which will be present for both of you.

You will experience a deep sense of gratitude, release and acceptance of each other and the contributions you brought to each other's life. Break out the champagne and toast to your successful journey through the ups and downs of your former relationship, each saying to the other, "so long for the time being."

My own personal experience

As I write these words, I flash back to some years ago when I was living in Australia. As a relationship guide, I was often a guest on national television, talking passionately about the benefits of a closing ceremony after the end of a relationship. Little did I know that I would soon have the opportunity to practice what I was preaching. Over the next three years, my own marriage went through a disintegration process and ultimately divorce. Vivienne and I had been together for 10 years and we had a son we loved very much. Even though there was tension between us and feelings of disappointment and anger, which often happens when a couple is finally separating, we mutually chose to walk away and close the door of our time together with gentleness and grace. I have no doubt that our decision to refrain from blame and detach our lives gently from each other had a positive impact on our son's emotional life.

About a year later, and after the initial challenging emotions had dissipated, we decided to do a closing ceremony to complete our time together. We were living in a beautiful place called Noosa, where the mountains slope down to the sea. So we drove to our favorite mountain with an easy drive to the summit and brought our gratitude list, a bottle of champagne, and a picnic blanket. As the sun set we poured ourselves a glass of champagne and alternated sharing from our lists of gifts received from each other during our relationship. It went on for over an hour as we both had a large list. Between the laughter, the tears, and our love, we said our goodbyes in the most direct and beautiful way. For me it was one of the most exceptional experiences of my life. Even though a part of us still had some residual negative emotions towards each other, I deeply appreciate our mutual choice to rise above those feelings and to end our relationship with dignity. For me, it felt amazing to receive her gratitude and appreciation for my contribution to her life. Now I know beyond the shadow of a doubt that the concept of closing ceremonies is a powerful process which enables a couple to bring the story of their relationship to completion in the most elegant way.

Partner who is totally closed to a completion ceremony – Many times a former partner remains stuck in the past, staying bitter towards you. Perhaps they're still blaming you for ending the relationship. The possibility of your former partner wanting to do a completion ceremony with you is slim. However, you still are able to create one for yourself.

Follow the above steps with the exception of you alone finding your place in nature to release your former partner with love. It's disappointing that your partner's consciousness is not at the same level of acceptance as you are and will not be present for your ceremony. In fact, by following through and performing your Closing Ceremony, you will release yourself and your partner from the cords to your past. Just read out loud your list of acknowledgments and the wind will carry them to your partner's heart. It may take two to make a relationship work but it only takes one to finally complete it.

Create a ceremony for all past partners – It's a very powerful process to release your former partners from the past. It's in your best interest to forgive and let go of resentments you may still be harboring toward any partners from your past by acknowledging their contribution to your life. There is a good reason for doing so. If we hold any bitterness or anger toward former partners then it's inevitable that those old stagnant emotions will negatively affect any relationship in your present experience.

It doesn't matter if you haven't heard from them in 20 years, just performing the Closing Ceremony for each one of them alone sets you free from the past. It will finally put closure to some important times in your life. If you feel safe to contact them and perhaps even send your list of acknowledgments to them with no expectations of any response, go ahead and do it. How would you feel if a former lover from years ago sent to you a list of gratitude for the positive contributions to their life? It would feel amazing that someone that once cared for you took the time and effort to reach out in time and space and thank you for your presence in their life.

Completion Ceremony for Widows/Widowers – Closing Ceremonies can also be a very effective tool for a widow or widower to fully acknowledge the positive contributions of their former partner to their life and assist in creating a sense of closure with that past relationship. Even though the deceased will always remain in the heart of the widow/widower, it's important for the sake of any future intimate relationship to refrain from elevating the memory of the deceased person to the level of sainthood. If we over-idealize our previous relationship, it will interfere in our ability to fully connect with a partner in any new relationship. A Closing Ceremony could serve as a beautiful way to bring a sense of completion to the widow/widower, while still allowing them to love and cherish the memory of the person they once loved and shared a life together.

New Horizons

It takes a good amount of maturity and life perspective to be able to complete this Closing Ceremony together. Looking forward, I envision a time when individual souls, ending their relationship, will rise above their petty grievances and deeply thank each other for their time freely shared while together here on Earth.

At the beginning of this 21st century, humanity typically ends relationships with resentment. The time will come when individuals, looking deeply into each other's eyes, will say "Thank you my friend for accepting my light and my dark, my joy and my pain and for giving me the two greatest gifts which you could have ever bestowed, your love and your time. We did the best that we could. Until we meet again."

Chapter 16

Serial Soulmates

People think a soulmate is your perfect fit, and that's what everyone wants. But a true soulmate is a mirror, the person who shows you everything that is holding you back, the person who brings you to your own attention so you can change your life.
Elizabeth Gilbert, (1969 -),
American Author of Eat, Pray, Love

I can't write a book about relationships and not delve into the subject of soulmates.

For most of us, when we think of the term soulmate, we conjure up images of the one and only person who was specifically made by the Creator just for us. Many people believe that a soulmate is our missing half. We often see a soulmate as that one person who completes us and is a perfect match to us on all levels, that is, physical, mental, emotional, and spiritual. For some individuals this may be so.

We often believe that when this one special being comes into our life, our life will magically become whole and that part of us which has felt incomplete will be fulfilled. We think that our soulmate is the missing link to our complete joy in life and when that soulmate arrives at our doorstep, life will become joyful beyond measure and we can leave all of our sadness behind.

Perhaps this is so. Perhaps not. For many years there was a part of me that certainly identified with the belief that my soulmate was the key to my happiness in life. In fact, there were a few times where I really believed I found my one and only soulmate. And then as time went by in the relationship and the inevitable challenges arose, I started to think that perhaps I didn't find my real soulmate and maybe she was still out there somewhere. After all, it's a common belief that when you are with your real soulmate, you aren't supposed to have any difficulties or arguments and if you do, you should be able to move through them with amazing elegance and grace. That was not what I was experiencing so the negative thought crept in that the woman I was committed to in a relationship was probably not my soulmate and I had made a mistake.

That is an awful place to find yourself, where you feel trapped in a relationship because you have the illusion that the person you are in a relationship with is not the soulmate that you thought they were. It's not good for you and it's certainly not good for the person who chose to be at your side. Yet many of us have at one time or another experienced a similar illusion.

So when did this concept of soulmate come into our collective consciousness? The first written documentation of the term soulmate was from the writer and poet Samuel Taylor Coleridge who wrote in a letter to a young lady in 1822, "To be happy in Married Life ... you must have a Soulmate."

Since then, we really don't see an increase in usage of the term soulmate until the 1960s, when the love generation, the baby boomers, were coming-of-age. The idealism of that renaissance generation increased the day-to-day usage of the term soulmate dramatically. Today it is commonly used to symbolize perfect love.

So where does this deep desire to be completed by another person in a soulmate relationship originate? Perhaps it's our souls desire to create wholeness in whichever way it can.

Referring to Chapter 12 Women and Men - Two Peas in a Human Pod, I see both men and women as often attempting to create wholeness within themselves by depending on their love interest to provide the missing parts of their nature that they have not developed within themselves. Many of us unconsciously seek out the missing parts of our own soul in the so-called soulmate. Until the man embraces the feminine aspects of his own inner being, he will seek out an external woman to express the feminine for him. And likewise, until a woman accepts her own inner masculine qualities, she will unconsciously seek out an external man to express the masculine for her.

In other words, our soul is wanting us to become whole beings by embracing the opposite aspects of gender within our nature, and when we resist this natural growth process, we will unconsciously lean heavily on the opposite sex to provide the very qualities that are absent and not developed within our own conscious nature. That's why we often feel so incomplete without our soulmate in our lives because up until now we may not have developed that wholeness within ourselves that our soul is searching for.

The very fact that we are searching for a Soulmate means that we have a soul that's doing the searching.

So that brings up the question "What is a soul and when did we get one?" —an impossible question to answer. Let's assume that we have a soul and that it existed prior to us coming here to this planet.

In saying that, many religions believe that a soul is a part of the Creator's Spirit and that we humans are given a freshly minted soul at birth. Other belief systems say that the soul has existed for eternity and takes on a human life for the growth of the soul through our experiences in human form.

Assuming the latter, what if, before our souls were born onto this Earth, we made agreements with various other souls to assist us with certain growth experiences while here so that our souls could develop, heal and grow in positive ways from those experiences? These agreements form a bond or soul connection with each soul to meet up at certain times during this lifetime to assist each other in becoming more whole. Some of those experiences would be joyful and some of them would be very painful; however all the lessons shared between those souls would be for their ultimate growth while here on Earth and a fulfillment of their promises to each other before they were born.

> I think most people have soulmates and don't realize it. Soulmates aren't just intimate love relationships. Soulmates can also be a parent, a sibling or friend.
> Even pets.
>
> Karen M Black,
> Author of Moondance

What if the group of souls that we agreed to meet here and spend differing amounts of time with while we are here on Earth are actually a type of soulmate? What if soulmates were not limited to romantic partners? What if your best friend or your daughter or your art teacher could be a soulmate? What if they were part of that group of souls who chose to spend time with us so that we can learn specific lessons for our personal growth and development?

Serial Soulmates are souls who agreed to contribute to each other's life by spending time together, for varying reasons, while here on Earth.

What if there were not only one soulmate for you, but several? What if there are actually Serial Soulmates who come into your life to assist you in rounding out your rough edges and learning to be a more complete human being?

Serial Soulmates are individual souls who have agreed to be with you for certain periods of time in order to assist you in learning a lesson, sharing love or just having a good time together while here on this amazing little planet called Earth.

When it comes to romantic soulmates, what if your most

challenging abusive relationship was actually a gift in that it was a soul who helped you learn how to stand up for yourself and become strong by no longer accepting abuse? What if that lesson assisted you in becoming healthier by learning to set boundaries with others? Even though it was a difficult lesson, wasn't that also a gift that you may not have received had that soulmate not made an agreement with you to assist you in learning to say no?

Perhaps soulmates are not limited to the romance department. Perhaps they can be specific souls who made an agreement to assist us to grow in some uplifting or challenging way while here on this planet.

A romantic partner or soulmate can only be a reflection who we are and as we heal the wounded parts of our nature and become more balanced, joyful and loving, then it's only natural that any soulmate who comes into our experience will reflect those same qualities right back to us.

As we develop into more complete beings by balancing the areas of our life that require our love and attention, then because of the law of attraction, which says that like attracts like, we attract into our experience a mate, partner or soulmate who is a mirror of our more balanced life. As we grow in our ability to give and receive love, we attract beings into our experience who are a reflection of us in that they are able to match our ability to love more profoundly.

Maybe that's how we arrive at the perfect soulmate —by the experiences and sacrifices of the former soulmates who helped us work out the rough surfaces of our personalities and character so that we would be in a better place to receive our greater good with a future partner.

A soulmate is the one person whose love is

> powerful enough to motivate you to meet your soul, to do the emotional work of self-discovery, of awakening.
> Kenny Loggins (1948-)
> Singer/songwriter

What if the person who may be standing at your side right now, although imperfect, is actually the perfect one for you and as you both learn your lessons through your own personal inner work, your current relationship may blossom into the soulmate connection you have always dreamed of?

If we can come to an understanding that a soulmate is not about having the perfect partner in life, it's about knowing that as we work on perfecting our own human self through personal growth on all levels, it's inevitable that whoever chooses to stand next to us shoulder to shoulder will be a perfect reflection of our new awareness and state of being. As you personally grow and learn to open our heart to the increased flow of love pouring through yourself and to others, the soulmate who dances at our side will give back to you in full measure the love you have learned to accept and share. It can be no other way.

> Forget not to show love unto strangers: for thereby some have entertained angels unawares.
> Bible, Hebrews 13:2

In my own life I know that I have had some powerful soulmate connections that have contributed greatly to my growth as a human being. To all my former relationship partners who may be reading these pages, you were my soulmate beyond the shadow of a doubt. We loved each other and exchanged many gifts even though some of those gifts were really challenging for us. Thank you for loving me in spite of experiencing some of the worst of me. Many of the gifts we shared were also amazingly joyful. I deeply thank you for the gifts of your love, time and presence in my life.

Chapter 17

Attracting a Life Partner

Many people believe that finding their true partner is like trying to find a needle in a haystack. With millions of possible choices out there, how will you find the one? You will find your partner by turning yourself into a powerful thought magnet. Then walk through the haystack of life and your "needle" will follow you home.

Des Coroy.

If you are not presently in an intimate relationship and would like to create one for yourself which meets all of your expectations, then this chapter will assist you in doing so. Before reading any further, I request that you bookmark this page and reread Chapter One, Raise the Level of Your Expectations. Refine the list of expectations you desire in a partner that you created for yourself at the beginning of this book. Add to your list any additional qualities that you would prefer in a partner.

One of the chief causes of the high divorce rate worldwide is a lack of overall compatibility between partners to begin with. In the initial rush of attraction, it's easy to confuse passion with compatibility. If you're not clear about the qualities you want in a partner, then the chances are you will attract the qualities you don't want.

There are four major reasons why the partner of your dreams is not standing at your side. Any one of the following reasons could sabotage the search for your partner:
1. Your lack of clarity about your needs and desires.

2. Your negative thoughts and beliefs about your ability to attract a partner who will match those requirements.
3. Settling for fewer qualities in a partner than you want because of your fear of loneliness.

4. Lack of self-worth because of your reluctance to develop within yourself the same qualities you would like to have in a partner.

You may think that in order to find a suitable partner, you have to assertively look far and wide for that special someone. Since potential partners are out there' you sometimes initiate a frantic house-to-house search to find your soulmate. Often you feel that time is wasting away and if you don't hurry up and find your unique one and only, you could wind up spending the rest of your life alone.

The pressure increases dramatically when you reach the dreaded '30-year panic. This is when your mother starts turning up the heat on you to grab the next breathing person who walks by, and to settle down and give her those grandchildren which are long overdue.

It's an inside job

If you don't have a clear picture of what you want in a partner, you could be searching for a long, long time. Your search needs to begin within your own heart and mind. As you mentally clarify the specific qualities you want in a partner, along with the power of your desire to find that partner, you take one large step toward the realization of your dream.

You live in a magical universe where the power of your thought creates your reality. Physicists will be the first to tell you that all matter is not as solid as it seems. Moving past the atomic level, everything material which exists is pure energy in motion, held together by the power of attraction. The Universe itself is a giant thought form of energy patterns in constant vibratory motion interacting with the most sublime intelligence. Before anything appears in this visible reality, the pattern or thought form must first be present.

The master architect of the universe, the Creator, uses thought as the bridge between spiritual creative power and physical reality. This mental program of the Creator, called Universal Creative Mind, is embedded in the entire physical structure of the universe. From the largest galaxy to the smallest atom, from the simplicity of a microbe to the complexity of a human being, everything that exists in physical form first pre-existed as a thought in Universal Creative Mind.

The power of your thought

One of the primary aspects of Universal Creative Mind is creativity. As offspring of this Creative Mind, you have the dynamic ability to mentally co-create through your Higher Mind the things in life which you desire. It is your spiritual heritage to do so.

We are what we think. All that we are arises with our thoughts. With our thoughts, we make our world.
Buddha, (568 - 488 BC), Founder of Buddhism.

Before anything shows up in human form it is first envisioned by the thought of the person creating it. The Sydney Opera House or the Pyramids of Egypt are magnificent physical structures which first appeared as a thought in the mind of the architect who designed it. Everything is the result of a thought. The car you drive, the house you sleep in, the jet you fly in. and the clothes you're wearing, all are the result of a thought from the person who designed it. The next great evolutionary leap forward for humankind will be a thorough understanding of our ability to mentally create the life that we envision.

How to Attract a Life Partner

1. Form a crystal clear thought of the specific qualities you would like your partner to have. You have the full ability to create the relationship that you visualize in your mind. Clarifying what your needs and desires are for a relationship is a very important step in bringing your relationship into reality. One of the major causes of mismatched relationships and their subsequent separation is that each partner's physical, emotional, mental and spiritual expectations are out of sync with the other.

Initially, opposites may attract because each partner provides qualities which the other needs. Everything would be okay if each partner developed the latent qualities in themselves which are fully present in the other. They would each grow toward each other and be enriched by the experience.

Because of the mirroring process in relationships, many people think they're opposite to each other and yet if they looked just a little deeper below the surface, they would see that they're much more similar than they would like to think. The problem with true opposites is that most individuals tend to polarize back into their own comfort zone and refuse to stretch in their partner's direction. For it to work, it takes a high degree of consciousness from each partner to grow the undeveloped aspects of their being. Because of completely different interests in life, a relationship of opposites will usually take them in different directions. They certainly won't be spending as much time together as a couple who are more compatible.

Couples who are more in tune with their expectations probably have an easier time creating harmony in their relationship. Similarities between partners means more time together because of compatible interests. Many life lessons are still to be learned between them. It's just that the bridge that spans the differences between them will be somewhat easier to cross. When spending time with a close friend, we usually choose individuals who are very similar to ourselves in values and desires.

By clarifying your expectations in a relationship you are much more likely to attract a partner who is your best friend and is very similar to you.

a) If you haven't yet refined your list of expectations for the type of relationship that you want, then do so now. Be as specific as you possibly can, remembering to write down everything you desire in a partner. Once you have made your list, put it away in a safe place and add or subtract items on it at any time. Keep your list of expectations completely private, even from your closest friends, as you weaken the power of your intention by sharing it with others.

b) Emotionally support your desire for your partner by allowing your feelings of anticipation and excitement to empower your thought. A clear thought without the energy of feeling is like an arrow without the bow. It is a combination of the two that propels your thought out into space and attracts your partner to you. Release your thought to the universe and trust that your good shall come to you in due time. Refrain from worry and move on with your life with the full expectancy that your thought and desire for your special partner will manifest at some point in your future. You've waited this long, so if it takes a little bit longer, so be it. Tell your mother that if she wants a grandchild so badly she can go adopt one.

2. Negative thoughts and fear repel the very partner you are seeking to attract. You create your reality with your predominant thought. If you're predominant thought is negative you will create a negative reality for yourself. It's as simple as that. Getting a clear vision about what you want in a partner is the first step.

Sustaining and protecting that vision is the second step. Your own negative thoughts and the negative thoughts of others will totally sabotage your dream if you don't consciously stand guard against the two. You do this by refusing to add any fear-based emotions to the negative thoughts which will occasionally pass through your mind.

This takes practice because we live in a fear-based culture with very low expectations about what's possible in a relationship.

Stay away from conversations with people who are negatively minded about the possibility of finding the right partner. Because of the past pain in your own life, you have parts of you which may attempt to sabotage your vision with negative thoughts from within. It's inevitable that you will have the occasional negative thought from time to time while you're waiting for your partner to come into your life. Just don't entertain those thoughts for any length of time. Let them pass through.

There is one very powerful phrase that you can use which will assist you in shifting from the negative when it occurs to the positive, and that phrase is, "up until now." It recognizes the validity of your past while still allowing for the creation of the new. "Up until now I have had pain and disappointment in my relationships. From this moment forward, with the assistance of Infinite Intelligence, all things are possible for me."

> *Every person, all the events of your life are there because you have drawn them there. What you choose to do with them is up to you.*
>
> Richard Bach, (1936 -),
> American author.

3. Be patient, maintain your vision and don't compromise it for any reason. Quite often, because of loneliness, we become impatient and lower the bar of our expectations and settle for a person that doesn't quite match the image we had in mind for a life partner. Don't be afraid of being alone for a while, if necessary, because to enter into a relationship that is far from the one that you have envisioned will postpone any possibility of emotional fulfillment.

You've put a lot of hard work into defining your relationship vision and then protecting it from mental negativity. Now is when you need to be vigilant, patient and steadfast in your faith that your partner will arrive in your life at the perfect time. If you want to have your visualization materialize, you must "knock the rust off your trust" and totally believe in your power to manifest exactly what you want. Inspirational books can support you with the encouragement you may need to persevere. Dr Wayne Dyer wrote a brilliant book which sums up the manifestation process called, *You'll See It When You Believe It*, which will certainly light a fire under your dreams.

Man, alone, has the power to transform his thoughts into physical reality; man, alone, can dream and make his dreams come true.
Napoleon Hill, (1883 – 1970), American speaker, motivational writer,
Think and Grow Rich.

4. Nurture in yourself the very same qualities that you're expecting in your partner. When you have a quiet moment, evaluate each quality on your expectation list in relation to yourself. Determine which expectations or values on the list are not being fully expressed in your own life. There are always qualities in life which we could strengthen within ourselves. Be honest with yourself but compassionate at the same time. We all have blind spots in our self-awareness where we could use a little effort. To expect qualities in a partner which are not present in our own nature is to invite disappointment.

You may be able to attract the partner that you desire because of the power of your thought, although you probably will not be able to hold them in your life because of a lack of resonance between you. If on a deep level you don't feel worthy of your expectations because of low self-esteem, in all probability you will not even attract your partner into your experience to begin with.

If you take the time to balance yourself physically, emotionally, mentally, and spiritually, you will develop within yourself the inner qualities that will match the inner vision of your partner to come. Remember, nothing is more attractive than inner self-confidence and self-acceptance. The personal growth in your awareness will prepare you to fully receive the gift of your partner's love. The day will come when you and your partner, standing side by side, will look into each other's eyes and with unspoken words whisper in your heart, "Hello my friend. It's good to see you again."

Know beyond the shadow of a doubt that what you are seeking, is seeking you

In your quest for a life partner for your dance through time, you'll have times of doubt and fear that the one for you may not come. I know of the deep longing in your heart to be with your long-awaited friend and the unexpressed feelings of sorrow because your partner is not yet present in your life.

When your faith waivers and you're losing hope climbing the steep hill of your dreams, there standing at the top is your Higher Self saying, "Come on my friend, just a little bit further. From here I can see that just over the next horizon, someone special is searching for you. Don't give up now because the difficulty of your journey will soon be forgotten. Just keep walking a little bit more, and everything will be all right."

Chapter 18

New Vision

Someday, after mastering winds, waves, tides and gravity, we shall harness the energy of love; and for the second time in the history of the world, man will have discovered fire.
Pierre Teilhard De Chardin (1881-1955),
French Mystic, Author.

Here at the beginning of the 21st century, we find ourselves living in a time of unprecedented personal and global change. Our most important relationship, our relationship with the very planet we live on, is being tested on every front.

It's clear that our planetary host, Earth, is going through a time of crisis unmatched in the historical record. I prefer to think of it as a healing crisis.

Faith energizes while fear immobilizes

In times of massive societal change, there is always a period of instability and uncertainty which is reflected on all levels of our world culture. Systems of every kind, whether biological, environmental, political or social, appear to be in a state of decay. Seeing the world through eyes of fear will only blind you to the actual transformation occurring around you. Fear sees decay while faith sees renewal. I'm sure the caterpillar has serious concerns while in the process of changing into a butterfly.

We are being challenged as a species to rise above our fear and use our intelligence and wisdom to safely navigate the global transformations that are now occurring. On the surface, things appear to be well out of hand, yet below the visible chaos, enormous tidal forces of evolution are at work shifting the future destiny of our planet onto a path of equilibrium. It's imperative that we see through the massive fog of fear clouding our vision by restoring our faith in our ability to turn things around. It is time for us to confidently step into the role of planetary custodian. All life forms are waiting to see if we will accept our collective responsibility for the health of our spinning world. I believe we will boldly answer the call.

Humanity's relationship with the Earth is a mirror reflection of our individual relationship with our own inner selves. If we are at war with the hated parts of ourselves, we will be at war with others. If we experience ill health and disease because of our refusal to balance our bodies with regular exercise, nutritious food and reduced stress, we will project our woes to the ailing biosphere of the planet. If we chemically pollute our bodies, we will pollute the very ground which sustains us.

On the other hand, as we begin to purify and heal our bodies, we will naturally purify and heal the planet. If we begin to accept, integrate and love the disowned parts of our nature, we will learn to accept our fellow women and men as kindred spirits in the same human family riding together in a spaceship called Earth.

As individual human beings begin to flower from the adolescent stage of our development into true adulthood, they will naturally form more harmonious relationships with their life partners, their children, other humans and ultimately with the planet itself.

Earth is supporting its own healing by attracting beings to its surface who are committed to transformation on all levels, personal, social and environmental. You are one of these beings, a rainbow warrior, who was attracted here to assist in the birth process of a New Era. You and many of your brothers and sisters on Earth at this moment are the true Marco Polos of consciousness, exploring inner awareness and creating a dynamic new renaissance with the power of knowledge inflamed with love.

If you want to change the world, change yourself. Start in the garden of your own heart. Strive to balance your life in all areas, physical, emotional, mental and spiritual. As you become finer tuned, the world becomes a little bit more stable. When millions of human beings across the globe achieve a greater state of equilibrium, the Earth will respond with a song of regeneration and peace.

Pro-creation expands into re-creation

As men and women assimilate within themselves the complementary qualities of the opposite sex latent within their own natures, they will see each other as true equals in this dance of life. Out of this equality a true communion of souls will be born.

Humanity is calling out for new examples of dynamically evolving partnerships of equality that will serve as a positive model for many couples to emulate. Creative energies will be liberated from these unions which will assist in the rejuvenation of our planet.

I see a time in the not too distant future where intimate relationships will be viewed as the sacred partnerships they were always destined to be. The day shall come when women and men, co-creators in life, will celebrate their togetherness with ongoing appreciation for the spiritual playmate who chose to stand at their side.

The more I think about it, the more I realize there is nothing more artistic than to love others.
Vincent Van Gogh, (1853-1890),
Dutch painter.

As independent human spheres revolving around their own axes, women and men will forever be surprised at the myriad unexplored facets of each other's nature. With increased awareness of the depth and complexity of the snowflake individuality of each other's soul, monotony transforms into exploration and ecstasy will become a way of life.

Thank you for joining me on a journey through the pages of this book. Until we meet again,

Des Coroy.

Appendix 1
Children and the Talking Stick

Children love the **Talking Stick** because it allows them the opportunity to speak their mind. The Talking Stick alleviates the problem mentioned earlier in this book of children not being heard by the adults in their life. They feel empowered in their ability to capture an adult's attention while holding the stick.

My son, Beau, once said, "When you have the Talking Stick, people listen to you more." We kept our Talking Stick in a place that was accessible to him. Any time he wanted to talk to us about something he felt was important, he used the Talking Stick and was able to communicate to us about his issue. The Talking Stick teaches children how to communicate with fairness and strengthens their ability to listen more effectively to others.

Family meetings

If there are important issues that need to be discussed with the family, the Talking Stick is a great tool to use in facilitating fair communication among everyone. It's a wonderful instrument for creating harmony within the family by allowing everyone's opinion to be voiced.

A good method to use would be for the family to sit in a circle. The individual who called the meeting speaks first about the issue and then passes the Talking Stick around the circle so that each person has an opportunity to speak. Bypass the feedback step. After every person has had an opportunity to speak once, place the Talking Stick in the center of the circle. Whoever feels inclined to speak can pick up the Talking Stick again to dialogue about the issue, and then return it to the center of the circle when finished. Stay with the process until everyone has at least an understanding of the issue, if not a genuine resolution of it. The freedom to speak without interruptions will give everyone an opportunity to be truly heard. Even the shyest members of the family will feel safe enough to voice their opinion and the ones who are most talkative will be silenced.

If a family member has an issue with a particular person then it's okay to shift into using the Talking Stick in the methods described earlier in this book where each person speaks for 30 seconds and then receives appropriate feedback from the listener. Remember, it's not always important to resolve an issue while having a Talking Stick session with another individual. Quite often, just the process of being able to speak and listen to each other about a particular problem will lay the groundwork for a future resolution.

Classroom use of Talking Stick

The Talking Stick is ideal for teaching children the benefits of listening to others in a school setting as well as encouraging them to participate more in the classroom by speaking their views. The teacher acts as a facilitator of the class by using the family meeting method previously mentioned of seating the students in a circle and then passing the Talking Stick around one by one. It can be used to have a class dialogue about geography, science, literature or any other subject which encourages each student to express their point of view.

The Talking Stick is increasingly being utilized in the Canadian school system as an effective communication tool for students.

Experiment with the Talking Stick in ways that suit your particular situation. Children love to hear about the origins of the Talking Stick in Native American culture and how it was used in the tribal councils as a symbol of the privilege of speech. Consider getting the students involved with constructing a Talking Stick using feathers, crystals or whatever else the collective class imagination can create.

Prevents bullying

Bullying is a major problem in school systems today. Every day, students are emotionally and physically abused in our classrooms. Often teachers are not clear on how to effectively stop it. Because the Talking Stick creates a sense of safety for children to speak up and be heard, it's a great way to tackle such difficult topics as bullying.

Using the Talking Stick, the teacher initiates a class dialogue about the destructive effects of bullying in general and gives each child an opportunity to express how they feel about such cruelty without naming any specific individuals in the class. It's very important to set a strong rule at the beginning of the session that no one is to visually or verbally identify any child in the class who bullies so as to avoid embarrassing or humiliating them. When aggressive children hear their fellow classmates share their feelings about bullying, peer pressure will often be enough for them to want to stop their misbehavior. It's especially powerful when the Talking Stick is passed to the children who bully others and then it becomes their turn to talk to the class about their own views on bullying.

Because children who bully prefer to do their damage in private, the Talking Stick gives the students the chance to publicly expose their feelings in the safety of the group.

Of course, bullying is a very complex problem which requires a range of possible solutions, but the Talking Stick provides teachers with a powerful communication tool in the fight against child-on-child harassment.

Appendix 2

The Talking Stick Method 2

Method 2: is a way of using the Talking Stick that encourages the expression of deeper feelings. I recommend using Method 2 only after you have had lots of practice with Method 1 and are comfortable with the process of equally sharing the Talking Stick. If there is relative harmony between you then this method can enable you to quickly get to the core of an issue.

Note: The only difference between Method 1 and Method 2 is the way in which each partner alternates speaking.

Here we have **Partner A** and **Partner B**:

Step 1: Partner A speaks first.
• **Partner A** holds the Talking Stick and speaks for a maximum of 20 seconds.
• **Partner B** listens attentively while not interrupting.

Step 2: Partner B summarizes and mirrors what was said back to Partner A.
• **Partner A** releases the Talking Stick after speaking for a maximum of 20 seconds by putting it on the table. This indicates to the listening partner that Partner A is finished speaking.
• **Partner B** summarizes or paraphrases what was heard and mirrors it back to Partner A and then asks for confirmation by saying, "Is that right?" (The reason for this is to determine if Partner B correctly heard what Partner A said.)
• **Partner A** answers the question, "Is that right?" in one of two ways.
  (1) If **Partner A** says, "Yes that's right," then **Partner A** again picks up the Talking Stick and continues to speak for another 20-second period, repeating Steps 1 and 2.

(2) If **Partner A** says, "No that's not what I said," then **Partner A** again picks up the Talking Stick and verbally repeats and clarifies what was originally said. After **Partner B** gets the message correct, then **Partner A** again picks up the Talking Stick and continues to speak for another 20-second period, repeating Steps 1 and 2.

Step 3: Partner A continues to speak in 20-second periods, repeating Steps 1 and 2, until she has completely expressed her point. Partner A then passes the Talking Stick to Partner B.

Step 4: Partner B now holds the Talking Stick and switches roles with Partner A by repeating Steps 1, 2 and 3.

Acknowledgments

To the many individuals who came to me for guidance, I deeply thank you for the experience of inviting me into your life and sharing your difficulties, dreams and joys. Your being has enriched these pages.

I am appreciative of Candace Apple, who gently but consistently nudged me into my healing work at a time when I needed a friend's encouragement to trust my gifts.

Heartfelt thanks to the wisdom of the Native American tribes who first created the Talking Stick long ago and preserved its power for the people of Earth.

Thanks to Shakti Gawain, for her practical revelations on the inner child, the mirroring process, voice dialogue and especially for providing me with a living example of someone who is successfully integrating the masculine and feminine parts of her being.

Additional thanks goes to James Wanless, whose dynamic expression of his inner Magician, Emperor and Chariot qualities through masterful communication inspired me to discover those very same qualities within myself.

To my dear sister, Judy, thank you for all the times in which you emotionally and spiritually supported me when my relationship experiments didn't quite work out as planned. You were always there for me.

Thanks to my brother, Marvin. Even though we have lived apart for so long, I have always felt the love and kindness of your soul.

To my mother, Eloise, thank you for teaching me emotional strength, faith, enthusiasm for life and how to tear up a dance floor. You have always believed in me and stood by my side in my darkest hours. I look forward to a champagne toast at your 100th birthday celebration. I love you. mom.

Warmest thanks to my Australian family, Vivienne

Acknowledgments

Somers, Peggy and Matthew Denham and Cal Arnesen and especially Judy Somers, for opening your hearts and inviting me in.

I give thanks for the wise young man in my life, my son Beau, who reminds me not to forget the little Des inside of me. Thank you for the many gifts that you have brought into my life. Remember son, "We never give up!"

Special thanks to my beautiful granddaughter, Taya, and my handsome grandsons, Cortland, Lyndon, Ean & Ellis for enhancing my life with your smiles. May the ideas in this book enrich the quality of your future relationships.

With the deepest gratitude of my soul, thank you to my three incredible daughters Kelly, Crystall and Vanessa for teaching me about love. I am totally honored for having the privilege of being your father this lifetime. You are all remarkable women and I wish you the most joyful journey on the seas of love.

And finally, a heartfelt thanks to the women of my life who chose to walk by my side on the path of intimate love. The lessons learned from our experiences together, all of them, including the rewarding and the challenging times, have greatly contributed to any insights or wisdom which may be in the words of this book. Thank you for the shared gift of your time.

For information about

Des Coroy

www.descoroy.com

Email: info@descoroy.com

Books, and general information can be acquired through this web site.

Des is available for speaking engagements and seminars and can be booked through his web site.

We would like to hear from you about your own personal stories from utilizing the concepts presented in this book.

Please ask for **Des Coroy's** products, **at Amazon.com** or your local bookstore.

Should you have any difficulty, contact us through our web site.

Internet Contacts of Authors Mentioned in this Book

The Path of Transformation by Shakti Gawain
The Relationship Handbook
www.shaktigawain.com

The Artist Way by Julia Cameron
www.artistswayatwork.com

Eat, Pray, Love by Elizabeth Gilbert
The Signature of all Things
www.elizabethgilbert.com

You'll See It When You Believe It by Dr. Wayne Dyer
www.drwaynedyer.com

Radical Forgiveness by Colin Tipping
www.radicalforgiveness.com

The Dark Side of the Light Chasers by Debbie Ford
www.debbieford.com

Recovery of Your Inner Child by Lucia Capacchione
www.luciac.com

Embracing Each Other by Hal Stone & Sidra Stone PhD
www.voicedialogueinternational.com

Managing Anger by Gael Lindenfield
www.gael-lindenfield.com

www.ingramcontent.com/pod-product-compliance
Lightning Source LLC
Chambersburg PA
CBHW051939290426
44110CB00015B/2034